COMPILED BY
JENNIFER BARDOT

Living Well
WITH
GRIT

You stumbled, yet you picked yourself up, and landed feet-first on solid ground. With greater confidence, you can now see your future on the horizon, and you know the next step to take.

LIVING WELL WITH GRIT
MDC Press

Published by **MDC Press**, St. Louis, MO
Copyright ©2024
All rights reserved.

All contributing authors to this anthology have submitted their chapters to an editing process, and have accepted the recommendations of the editors at their own discretion. All authors have approved their chapters prior to publication.

Cover, Interior Design, and Project Management:
Davis Creative Publishing, DavisCreativePublishing.com

Writing Coach and Editor: Pam Wilson

Compilation by Jennifer Bardot

Publisher's Cataloging-in-Publication
Names: Bardot, Jennifer, compiler.
Title: Living well with GRIT / compiled by Jennifer Bardot.
Description: St. Louis, MO : MDC Press, [2024]
Identifiers: ISBN: 979-8-9918970-0-6 (paperback) | 979-8-9918970-1-3 (ebook) | LCCN: 2024923036
Subjects: LCSH: Courage--Literary collections. | Courage--Anecdotes. | Resilience (Personality trait)-- Literary collections. | Resilience (Personality trait)--Anecdotes. | Perseverance (Ethics)-- Literary collections. | Perseverance (Ethics)--Anecdotes. | Self-realization in women-- Literary collections. | Self-realization in women--Anecdotes. | Well-being--Literary collections. | Well-being--Anecdotes. | LCGFT: Anecdotes.
Classification: LCC: BJ1533.C8 L58 2024 | DDC: 179.6--dc23.

Dedication

*To all the selfless individuals
learning to put themselves first:*

*The familiar sayings,
"Put on your own oxygen mask first," and
"You can't pour from an empty cup" only
resonate when we truly recognize
the value of self-care.*

*This book is dedicated to those
who are bravely prioritizing themselves,
setting boundaries, standing up
for what they need, and embracing
a life they genuinely love.*

Table of Contents

Continued on next page

Additional Authors

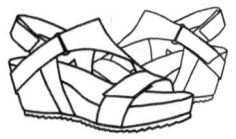

Jennifer Bardot

Learn, Evolve, Live Well

"Wisdom is not a product of schooling
but of the lifelong attempt to acquire it."
– Albert Einstein

I choose to live well by learning from life's lessons. Lessons are how I have gained the wisdom to learn more about myself and to discover what living well meant to me. It's through this journey I learned how to navigate through my past, taking me to the present, where I stand on a firm foundation. It's the wisdom I acquired through observing and interacting with others, evolving self, gaining education, and choosing to be vulnerable. Everyone has a perception of what living well looks like, and it evolves over time, yet can be learned at any age.

There came a time in my life when I knew something needed to change. I found myself surrounded by narcissists in all aspects of my life. I allowed myself to give trust to those who didn't deserve it, be disrespected, and be taken advantage of, which impaired my ability to listen to my intuition. It was at this pivotal time I made the hard choice to choose me. Although everything appeared to be ok from the exterior, I felt numb, sad, and empty. My body began giving me signs as I developed digestive issues, trouble sleeping, my hair began to fall out, and my anxiety was at an all-time high.

How had I allowed myself to get to this point? It was time to change the way I had been doing life. My anxiety had me taking baby aspirin and wearing compression socks. This difficult time forced me to ask for help and meet myself where I was each day. After visiting the doctor for what I thought was a blood clot, I found myself on a higher dosage of anxiety medication. I didn't know how much I was struggling until I found myself still in bed late in the afternoon, 2 p.m. to be exact. As an early riser, I knew something was wrong. I forced myself to take a shower and keep my virtual meetings but respected where I was at that moment and turned off my camera.

I became hyper-intentional, choosing to live well each day, surrounding myself with a genuine support system, monitoring my energy, and knowing when I needed to shift to positivity, have gratitude, and eliminate toxicity. Additionally, I had to learn how to go against my grain and advocate for what I believed was right. I had to learn to calm my emotions and be assertive and direct with those who had disrespected me. As a non-confrontational, reforming people pleaser, advocating for myself was uncomfortable but necessary for survival. The world that I had previously known was now spinning out of control and demanded me to retrain my brain to keep moving ahead daily. Constant triggers required me to be pushed out of my comfort zone and grow quicker than I had desired. These wounds began feeling as though I couldn't keep up with the bleeding, and I was fading fast. Yet I knew where our attention goes our energy flows, so I had to stop the hemorrhaging.

The bandages I used to heal were from monitoring my energy, taking naps, pulling back from certain activities, and being with people I love and who love me. Once scars developed from my wounds, I saw that I had been programmed to listen to negative self-talk and believe the inner voices in my head, stating that I didn't have value, nor was I enough. For every negative comment, it takes five positive thoughts to counteract. As I struggled for months, I found myself recovering quicker from these constant, unpredictable blows. By listening to my inner voice, I was able to gain the strength to keep going and live day by day. I realized the ebb and flow of life was out of my control, but my energy and joy were not. No matter how hard the struggle, I learned that I must dig deep, cry, talk, write, get angry, and then cry again, and the sun will always rise again. The friction that I have encountered along my journey has transformed this raw diamond into a unique and precious gem by owning my G.R.I.T.

Here are a few "Jennifer Bardot Signature" gems that I rely on.

Observation

Observing and interacting with others is how I have gained insights into what I perceive living well to look like. I've learned about myself through watching and interacting with others. This concept is called "mirroring," and it is a theory that illuminates hidden aspects of our behavior and identity, providing an introspective lens into the complexities that make up your unique self. This is a concept that sheds light on differences and similarities that allow you to have more self-awareness through interacting with and observing others. Engaging in conversations with others is another way for you to learn about yourself and what you enjoy. Developing self-awareness is how you begin to build the life of your dreams, allowing you to reach the peak of happiness. Watching and engaging in conversations with others helped me to understand how I wanted to design my life.

Stay Rooted

Staying grounded by never forgetting where you came from is an aspect of how I define living well. Have you ever heard of a concept called "Earthing"? It is when you peel your shoes off and plant your bare feet into the earth, walking in the dirt and grass. This concept of grounding is good for your body and significantly reduces stress. By remaining grounded in who we are and embracing our roots, we become the truest versions of ourselves, reducing stress. Choosing to live a grounded life allows you to build a foundation in self-realization, gratitude, and humility, truly listening to your inner voice and choosing to know who you are. Do you remember where you came from? Do you feel like you know yourself? Wisdom can be gained through personality tests, conversations, observations, and experiences, but it also comes from recalling the previous steps in your memories that have shaped you into the person you are today.

Story

At 18 years old, I was overly confident, but that quickly changed when faced with tremendous rejection. All my peers had been accepted into university; I, however, was denied from every institution I applied to. With the pile of rejection applications, I was quickly humbled, which taught me a lesson I carry with me today: Never allow yourself to get overly confident and assume all things will work out as you envision. To live well, you can't be arrogant. Even though I gained much wisdom from a path of failure through rejection, it motivated me to do better. I started with my associate's degree, transferred to complete my undergraduate degree, then two master's degrees and several certificates. This personal setback allowed me to see I desired more from my life. Through failure, I was able to set a goal and achieve higher academic standards.

Experiences

Experiencing failures, setbacks, transitions, successes, and advantages are the experiences we encounter that help us recognize when life is good. It is life experiences that allow us to transform our past and step into our future. While some experiences lead us to failure and others lead us to success, through each experience, we gain wisdom.

Choosing to learn from our failures is how we break cycles, change generational patterns, and create the life we dream of. We must own our mistakes to live wiser. By intentionally learning from my mistakes, I've made a choice not to repeat old, unhealthy patterns and become a better version of myself. It is a daily choice to break unhealthy patterns and to be intentional with my thoughts, actions, and choices in my life. Daily I rely on my support system, have gratitude for my journey, and choose to always evolve. In the remaining years of my life, I will not allow my ego to prevent myself from being open to all the possibilities of my life. Learning by doing is a great way to push yourself out of your comfort zone, but learning by doing and then choosing to do better is the way to become a wiser you. Get curious and you will learn more about yourself when you think through what led you to that experience or what you gained from that encounter. Understanding yourself is critical to choosing to live well so you can live authentically.

Vulnerability

By being truly honest with yourself, you will see areas you can improve, change, or maintain. By exercising this practice, I was able to realize that each day will never come again. We can continue to ignore it by keeping our blinders on from reality or face reality, which could lead us to better days ahead. Embrace the *now*! This is a way of life I now own. We can't go backward; we can live well every day forward. Tomorrow is never promised. Choosing to enjoy the now is within your control. Discovering a voice, setting boundaries, valuing a support system, and acknowledging where I have come from are how I choose to live well while being honest with myself. One of my favorite quotes is from Eleanor Roosevelt, *"Yesterday is history, tomorrow is a mystery, today is a gift. That's why we call it the present."* When you are honest with yourself, you are less likely to get smoked in the face with a brick but more likely to have bricks as your foundation as you walk strong and purposefully forward. The more in tune you are with yourself the more success you will have navigating forward.

Challenge

I challenge you to reflect: Have you experienced any event that has impacted *you*? Did this experience alter your future steps? Or did you continue making the same choices, getting the same results? Now is a time for you to change each day moving forward. Take this time to identify your patterns, triggers, unhealthy choices, and successes to uncover your perception of what living well means to *you*.

Jennifer Bardot, MA, MS, is a publisher and author of the *Deconstructing GRIT Collection* and *Owning Your G.R.I.T.*—five international bestselling anthologies available at Target, Walmart, Barnes & Noble, and Amazon. She is featured on the cover of St. Louis Small Business Monthly as 2021's "Top 100 Persons to Know to Help Grow Your Business," was awarded the President's Circle by Enterprise Bank & Trust, received the Titan 100 honor in 2024, was named one of the 2024 Most Influential Women in Construction by the National Association of Women in Construction (NAWIC), and has been seen on NBC, ABC, CNN, Fox2, and other media platforms. Founder of the GRIT Community—a free women's leadership group with over one thousand members—Jennifer holds a BA and dual master's degrees, has an active life and health insurance license, holds certificates in the Dare to Lead Training by Brené Brown, and has participated in Women in Leadership and Leadership St. Louis by FOCUS St. Louis. She served as a mentor for Lindenwood University, St. Louis University, Washington University, and Fontbonne University. She is the Leukemia & Lymphoma Society visionary in 2024. Jennifer is passionate about supporting business owners and leaders, is a dedicated mother to three boys, and is an outdoor adrenaline adventurer.

Please scan the QR code to connect with this author.

Karen Maurer

Exposed: The Courage to Share My Story

"I don't love you like a husband should love a wife." In that moment, my world shattered. After nine years of marriage and two children, my best friend and college sweetheart revealed he was gay. I was frozen…utterly speechless.

Moments after hearing the news, my tear-filled eyes looked at my confused children, and all I could feel was helplessness. The life I envisioned with my two- and four-year-olds had suddenly vanished. My dreams of giving them siblings were now shattered. What had just happened? My sense of security crumbled, leaving me consumed with grief, loneliness, and helplessness. This was too heavy to bear alone—especially with Mother's Day just around the corner.

In this moment, all I could say was, "I need to leave, but I will come back." I left the house and jumped in my car, not sure where I was going to go. I don't know how it happened, but "Jesus took the wheel," and I ended up sitting in the back row of our church. In that quiet space, I asked for help, strength, and resilience. I surrendered everything to God. This challenge was too big for me to handle on my own, and I desperately needed help. Surprisingly, I started to feel the darkness lifting from my body. I physically felt the weight of this news evaporate. In its place, I felt the need to accept and give grace. I felt stronger, more courageous. With this mindset, I knew I could be brave enough to push through the days ahead. I could move forward with intention and build the life I believed I was meant to live. I got in my car and drove home, ready to take the next step.

From there, we created a plan to separate but would prioritize the well-being of all of us. We were committed to maintaining our relationships with our extended families and friends, so we shared the news with everyone together. We made it clear that while people were free to hold their own views on homosexuality, negative comments would not be tolerated around our children. We knew we needed to be aligned and have an intentional plan. We would not tolerate people tarnishing his good reputation in front of the children. Although not everyone accepted our situation easily, I am proud to say that both of our immediate families eventually embraced our terms. Today, we all see each other frequently, and the children are very close to everyone. We knew we did the right thing and turned a very difficult situation into one that was handled with honesty and grace.

At the same time, I was dedicated to building a career in the financial planning industry. It was my professional dream, and I had been working toward this for many years. After serving as an administrative assistant to an advisor for nine years, I was ready to bloom. I had earned my certifications and licenses on my own time, fueled by determination and ambition. I eagerly awaited the promised paraplanning position when I returned from maternity leave with my son. But, when I walked in on that first day back, I was blindsided to discover they had hired someone else.

Two days later, I gave twelve weeks' notice. Why twelve weeks? I wanted to give the advisor ample time to find a replacement that I could train and ensure a smooth transition for him. I felt bitter, but not that bitter. I didn't want the transition to be difficult for him and his clients. I simply realized that I needed to grow, and the opportunity I needed wasn't available to me there. I wasn't going to waste time. If I couldn't find fulfillment in that environment, I would create a space where I could thrive, serve, and foster education and growth for my team. I vowed never to treat anyone the way I had been treated.

I left that company, and, along with an advisor also leaving, we launched our own financial advising firm. I refused to let anyone else dictate my future; I was determined to take charge of my own destiny! About a year later, I went through the aforementioned divorce. I was running a business in its infancy with no steady income, managing home expenses, caring for my two young children, navigating a lease and the salary of an assistant. Thankfully, I had $30,000 after the divorce, and that would buy me a little time to bring in clients and start generating an income. I wasn't afraid. I felt invigorated—tenacious, fired up, and ready for the challenge. Failure was not an option.

When I left my previous firm, I was offered the opportunity to take on eleven clients who no longer fit their ideal profile. Those eleven clients meant everything to me, and I devoted myself to providing them with exceptional attention, service, and gratitude. To this day, many are still with me, while others I have sadly accompanied on their final journeys. It's hard to believe that twenty-five years have passed since I started that firm.

I didn't do this alone; my parents supported me in every possible way. My father took on tasks around the new house that were outside my expertise, picking my children up from daycare and always treating them to their favorite snacks—memories they cherish to this day. My mom helped me organize, clean, and care for the kids, all while encouraging my independence as a mother and reassuring me that they were there if I stumbled. Their unconditional support taught me the importance of balance. They often took us on driving trips across the country, helping me realize I was just a small part of a vast and wonderful world. They ignited my passion for travel, a love that my children have inherited as well.

After a couple of years, I was ready for love again. I longed for the connection that a married couple should share. I met a man from England while in Puerto Vallarta, and we embarked on a whirlwind romance that took us to England, Switzerland, and Ireland. Eventually, he moved to the U.S., and we married. He had never been married before and didn't have children, so I don't think he was fully prepared for the reality of our blended lives.

Over the years, I discovered that our cultural differences and our ideals about family, religion, charity, and the future were not in sync. I wish I had recognized this sooner. As time passed, we grew increasingly apart, and he became angry and resentful. For my own sanity, we led very independent lives; to this day, I don't think he even knew what I did for a living. He pursued his interests while my children and I focused on ours. After a series of eye-opening and troubling incidents, I realized I didn't want to live this way for a lifetime. Fifteen years was enough. I would rather be alone than subject myself, my children, and my future grand-children to this environment. I chose myself. I chose my children. I chose to stand up for my well-being. And so, we divorced.

I felt a deep sense of shame and embarrassment—and I still do. Telling people about my second divorce without offering an explanation left them wondering: Who was at fault? What happened? I worried about how this would affect my credibility with clients and within my community. I've shared the reasons for my first divorce with very few people until now, and I prefer to keep the details of my second one in the past. My children feel the same way.

I knew I had to keep moving forward, growing with intention and purpose, and living a life filled with gratitude. I refused to let this negative experience dictate my future. Instead, I drew strength from my decision and used it as fuel to propel myself forward—quickly.

The kids and I embraced a fresh start that felt invigorating. My daughter had graduated from college and decided to continue her education in nursing, while my son was about to leave for college but would be staying in town. Both were (and still are) fiercely protective of me, and I cherished having them around frequently. My parents, as always, provided invaluable support, giving me the strength and courage to push forward with unwavering determination. After all, I loved financial advising—and still do—and I wanted to extend my impact to more people.

I also began living a much more grateful life. Had I remained in an administrative role at my previous firm, I wouldn't have had the freedom to be there for my children—picking them up on sick days, staying home during their time off, traveling, and attending their sporting events. I am forever grateful that I didn't get that job. I was finally living a balanced life, but something was still missing. I felt a strong desire to devote time and resources to a charity. After doing some research, I chose the St. Louis Crisis Nursery, knowing my passion for helping children.

My cup was full, often overflowing, especially when I was honored by them as Woman of the Year. I am honored to have served in various roles on the board at the Nursery, including President, and am now a lifetime board member. It is one of the most rewarding aspects of my life.

While I was enjoying a full and rich life, I realized I missed the blessing of a partner's love and the opportunity to love in return. So…I took a risk and put myself "out there." Yes, Match.com! And can you believe I met my true love? After his profile made me laugh aloud, I agreed to meet for a drink and several years later, we married. Brian brings me joy, purpose, and an instant family with six more children and ten grandchildren! Brian is the yin to my yang; he keeps me from being too serious and encourages me to slow down and take a breath. He made me a promise of "2+2+2." Every day, he sings me two songs, tells me two new stories, and makes me laugh with two jokes (yes, he actually does this!). Every woman deserves this kind of joy in her life.

We are grateful for every moment we share. Our intention to build a life together has introduced us to new hobbies like golf and scuba diving, all while fostering a shared commitment to treating everyone with dignity and respect. We built a home that welcomes family—both past and future generations. Together, we create new experiences through travel and cherish the world where we live and now thrive.

Throughout the challenges of my journey, my business experienced significant growth, driven by my mantra: "Do the right thing for the right reasons, and the money will follow." Helping others understand and achieve financial security has been incredibly rewarding, and on multiple occasions, I have been asked to speak about this and other topics. I never imagined I would be the one others sought out for guidance, but that's what was happening, and I knew that's where I belonged!

I am grateful for the successful business I've built and continue to grow. My experiences have taught me the importance of relating to my clients with empathy and compassion, allowing me to forge meaningful relationships. In the community, I've discovered a vibrant network of empowered women and men who are equally dedicated to connecting, learning, and thriving together. Through our mutual support, we enhance not only our own businesses but also the holistic care we provide to our clients.

Reflecting on my journey, I realize that life is about trust. Trusting that what may seem like a setback is often an opportunity for significant growth, even if it takes time to recognize. Trusting in my strength, resilience, and ability to inspire others. Trusting that I will never lose sight of the support I've received along the way. Trusting that by being vulnerable and sharing my story, I might help someone else. Trusting that I am exactly where I am meant to be. And ultimately, trusting in my capacity to continue growing with resilience, intention, and tenacity.

Karen is a seasoned Certified Financial Planner® and the founding partner of her original financial advisory firm, established in 1999. With 25 years of experience in the industry, she has cultivated a nationwide practice built on trusted client relationships. Recently, Karen has joined forces with Krilogy, a partnership that reflects her core values of respect, integrity, and a commitment to elevating the client experience.

Dedicated to a holistic approach to financial planning, Karen offers comprehensive services that encompass investment, insurance, tax, and estate planning advice tailored to individuals and couples. Her passion for education shines through in her role as a sought-after public speaker, where she shares insights on various aspects of personal financial management.

In addition to her professional endeavors, Karen is deeply committed to her community. She serves as a lifetime board member for the St. Louis Crisis Nursery and is actively involved in organizations such as the St. Louis Forum, the Creve Coeur Chamber of Commerce, Little Black Book, and various local women's organizations focused on personal and professional development as well as philanthropy.

Karen's dedication to her clients and community makes her a respected leader in the field of financial planning.

Please scan the QR code to connect with this author.

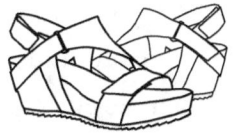

Erin Hamilton

Reinventing the Rules My Way

I have come to understand that we all need to make sure that we've lived a life we are proud of. A life worth remembering. To make thoughtful choices so that when we look around, we know our intentions have served us well.

As for me, my life isn't turning out the way I thought it would. It feels like I am supposed to say that, but deep down, I think it is going exactly like it was supposed to. It has just taken a lot of "undoing" the lessons I was taught from an early age. I grew up in a very midwestern household. My parents came from small, rural, middle-American towns and moved to the Chicagoland area before I was born. They brought with them a set of prescribed rules for a healthy, happy, and productive life.

I'm not sure if these guidelines for living were ever articulated as *rules*, it was just the way things were, and they were deeply ingrained. There was but one path. Who wrote these rules? I don't know, but I followed them anyhow. I studied and worked hard in high school to earn myself a full-ride scholarship to a Big Ten University. I managed to keep that scholarship (it was a struggle at times!) and earned the degree. After graduation, I threw in a plot twist, surprising everyone when I enlisted in the Air Force. It was a tumultuous time in our country, and I wanted to help. I *needed* to help. It was my first time *really* veering from the natural order I was to follow.

I loved everything about my time in service. I learned so many things about teamwork, leadership, friendship, and myself. I learned how to push through the tough and accomplish the even tougher. I had career goals and went to graduate school while working full-time. It was an extraordinary period for me. And alas, I had gotten the "order" back on track when my boyfriend and I announced our engagement. Timeline still intact. Phew.

After the wedding, we made the decision that I would not reenlist. We wanted to start a family and the job we did was not a great one for a young mother. Too many dangerous deployments were in the near future and not worth the risk if I was going to be someone's mom. We moved back to my husband's small town, got regular jobs, and started our family. We saved our money and built our forever home on a little corner of the family farm. I held my two boys in my arms, I took them on adventures, and then I watched my oldest walk away from me with a tiny backpack as he started school. I did not stray from the prescribed order of life and believed that all would go as planned. Until it didn't. Here I was again, falling outside of those rules. Now I'm the divorced one. *"Fantastic," I thought.*

I distinctly remember one evening, shortly after settling into our new house (just the three of us) and I needed to hang the backpack rack. I designated a place for it, by the garage door between the kitchen and the laundry room. I brought the shelf in from the garage where it had been left after our hasty move, got out the tape measure and a pencil, and stared at the wall. It was at that moment that I realized that I'm the only adult in the house. I'm it. Just me. When the bills need to be paid and the grass needs to be cut, it's on me. When it's time to make food or do laundry or any of the other million things it takes to keep a house running, it's only me. My boys were three and six years old and needed so much of my time still. How on earth was I going to do all of this? And I really had no idea how to hang a backpack rack so that all their books didn't rip the drywall right off the studs.

I had no family nearby, and I felt so much shame and embarrassment at being the divorced mom. I worried that the kids in school would tease my kids, that all Christmases would be forever ruined, and the neighbors would shun us. How little I knew back then. But while I didn't have much at the time, I had a whole lot of fire and grit. And an enormous sense of responsibility. I thought to myself…I signed up to be these boys' mom, and I would walk to the end of the earth to make sure that they had a peaceful and loving home. And as it turned out, my neighbors were amazing and supportive human beings who didn't give a second thought to my failed marriage. They just saw a girl who could use a hand, and they gave her one.

Professionally, I was always a bit of a renegade. I was often given harsh feedback and constantly handed development opportunities to improve. Again and again.

Truthfully, I got my ass kicked at work. All. The. Time. While part of me wanted to be petulant and resentful, the smarter part of me knew that no one would put this amount of effort into someone if they didn't see potential. I was told I wasn't polished and professional enough. I needed to "exec up." I needed to "tone down my communication style." I needed to "stop being so funny." (What kind of feedback is that? Who doesn't like to laugh?) This was so frustrating because I've always been highly competent and "got stuff done." What more did the world want from me? It felt like nothing I did was ever good enough. Despite my best efforts, competence, and rule-following, I just felt like I was failing at home and at work. It was maddening and confusing.

During a significant rough patch of introspection and professional development, I had a conversation with one of the best leaders I've ever had the privilege of working for. I explained to him my confusion and wondered why it always felt like I was being held to a higher standard.

Why, while being a top performer on the team, was perfection expected out of me when I could see others all around me behaving poorly without so much as a second glance? He told me, "Erin, not everyone defines things in the same way. From my perspective, professionalism is defined as someone who is who they say they are, does what they say they are going to do, and follows through. And you are one of the most professional people I've ever met. Just keep being who you are and showing up just as you are, and remember, the cream always rises to the top."

It was on that day that I decided I would always choose to do good things from a place of positive intent. I would maintain my integrity, my work ethic, and my version of professionalism. I would show up as myself, and if it wasn't good enough, I'd find somewhere that it was. This became the backbone of "who I am" as a professional. I'm me. And if that's not right for you, that's ok. It's right for somebody. I refused to spend another minute of my life pretending to be something I am not to fit into someone else's box. Or to follow someone else's rules.

I ended up leaving my long-term employer and starting the next step of my career advancement—finding organizations that needed real help to fix major problems. Organizations that would appreciate my can-do attitude and fierce tenacity to get the job done. Organizations that needed someone who was willing to challenge them beyond their status quo and make noticeable differences. I found it to be a space in which I thrived. I was able to push the boundaries because that was exactly what I was hired to do! It wasn't always fun or comfortable, but it was necessary, and I was good at it.

A few years later, I was in a new, happy relationship. He was a good role model for my kids and a really fun partner. We started a purified water delivery business together that is still growing to be incredibly successful. I was still managing my full-time career during the day and running our business in the evenings and on weekends. We moved into our dream home, and finally (finally!) I was living life the way it was "supposed" to go. Whew. Until again (again!) it wasn't. The pandemic happened. Life for a human resources leader trying to manage a manufacturing plant through a pandemic was unimaginably hard. Everyone was panicked and looking to me to know the answers when nobody knew the answers. I had to figure it out, and I had to do it fast. Meanwhile, I had to reassure my now 1,000 water customers that we would continue to deliver safely. And manage the giant upswing in business we got as a result of big box stores running out of water. It was great for business, but terrible for my time management skills that were barely hanging on.

And let's not forget the 2,000 other things that needed to be done, such as keeping kids engaged on Google Classroom and making sure everyone was fed daily. I was managing so many things at one time that I didn't even notice at first that I was doing it all by myself. I was getting no help and eventually was deemed "not fun enough." It shouldn't have surprised me that he created a new life with a new person and left our family in the dust, but it rocked me to my core. Overcoming betrayal, coupled with the integral feelings of never being enough, was the hardest experience of my life. I was the divorced one. Again. Looking back now though, it really was a blessing in disguise. I wasn't me when I was there. I was giving all of myself to someone who didn't even notice, just so that I could hang on to these ridiculous notions that I'm only a good mom if we live in the same house forever. I'm only a good mom if I'm married forever. I'm only a good mom if I make dinner every night. I felt trapped inside of a tiny box full of giant expectations. And I had had enough. So, I shredded that box into a thousand pieces and walked away, taller and stronger, to go find myself back.

All of this to say, I've had my fair share of heartache and disappointment. A girlfriend of mine told me once, "I don't know how you do it. I would be a puddle of goo by now if I went through half of this."

But over the years, I've learned a few things, and I've rewritten the rules. *My* rules. While we can't do any of this on our own, it is crucial to have an overwhelming belief in yourself. We don't owe the best of ourselves to anyone but ourselves. And it is absolutely necessary to walk away from any relationship that isn't serving you, no matter how much time and effort you have invested in that person. The most important relationship you will ever have is with yourself. Get to know you and who you really are and who you want to become. Figure out what serves you, and let the rest go. We don't have time for nonsense. I had to let go of thoughts of permanency. I realize that I'm happiest when I'm constantly reinventing myself based upon my needs of the current time. And we certainly don't have time to waste trying to squeeze ourselves into someone else's box.

I followed the rules. I still don't know who made them or why they even existed in the first place, so now I make my own. I've never been more happy or productive.

Erin Hamilton has nearly 20 years of experience in human resources practice and strategy, currently serving as the Executive Director of People and Culture at Caritas Family Solutions, a nonprofit organization dedicated to strengthening families and communities. Based in the St. Louis metro area, Erin focuses on leadership coaching, talent development, and organizational culture, fostering environments where individuals and teams thrive. She is also the proud owner of Honest Water, a growing purified water business start-up. Erin enjoys contributing to her community and has formerly held board positions and served as an elected city official. Passionate about purposeful intention and self-care, Erin integrates these principles into both her personal and professional life. She also enjoys reading, physical fitness, exploring the outdoors, and mastering jigsaw puzzles. As a mom to two teenage boys, she balances her roles with grace, bringing a nurturing yet strategic perspective to all she does.

Please scan the QR code to connect with this author.

Amanda Schroeder

GRIT Takes a Village

When I sat down to write my chapter in this anthology, I thought a lot about what I have been through in my life and career. Countless events came rushing to the forefront of my mind when I started brainstorming, and I realized that these experiences, while not extraordinary, are deeply relatable to many. The tenacity that drives us to move forward and continue to add value in each situation and circumstance we touch binds us together, just like the pages of this book. Many women in this anthology and the ones before have survived and endured more significant challenges than I will ever know, yet we all have a thread in common: grit. I then began to realize that each of us has reached this very point in our lives by different paths but with supporting voices littered along the route.

Instead of reliving particular metamorphic challenges in my own life (because just like anyone else, of course, there have been many), I wanted to take these few pages to pay homage and recognize those who have been in my corner throughout the way—the "men and women behind the curtain" whose very presence and existence provided solace and comfort in the darkest times of my life. Without their support, championing, constant encouragement, and even sometimes negative interactions, I could not imagine where I would be. Hopefully, by reading what

I have gained from those who have shaped me as an individual, you will look at your village and see the same impact on your own life.

It starts with the people responsible for shaping us in our early and formative years: our parents. I'm fortunate to have a group of parents and grandparents who have challenged me in many ways. My childhood was far from perfect, but each one did everything they could to help me understand the overarching theme of growing up: it gets better. My mother taught me that I could do anything, and I mean *anything,* if I gave it my best effort. My father taught me that the best things came wrapped in the ugliest paper and were often disguised as manual labor. My stepparents taught me that love can come from unexpected places that end up being some of the best things to happen to you. And my grandparents taught me that everything changes eventually, and learning how to adapt to that change makes you stronger with every challenge you face.

Every misstep I made throughout my childhood and teenage years could be met with any one of them explaining where I went wrong and how to do better next time. While at the time it may have been incredibly frustrating (and annoying, I'll be honest), it truly shaped who I am today in a way that paved a path of success for me as an adult. Knowing how headstrong I am as a mother, leader, and executive, I can only imagine how difficult my youth was for this group of people; however, without them, I would not have learned the basic principle of perseverance that I can only hope to pass on to my own children.

As difficult as I was as a child, I can't even imagine what it must be like to be married to a stubborn, driven, and strong-willed woman like me. I have completed three degrees as a married mother and am working toward my fourth, even after just welcoming my fourth child into the world. I have realized the toll that being tenacious in your career and education can take on a marriage, and without proper attention and care in your relationship with your significant other and partner, it can have devastating consequences. The support from my husband has been unwavering, to say the least, and without it, I would most certainly crumble from pressure. While I do not doubt I could overcome any challenge in my life and career, his strength, support, and encouragement drive me to meet these obstacles gracefully. His continual question of "What's next?" is frequently in my mind as I consider the next steps in my career and education, and for that, I love him deeply and more than either one of us could ever fully understand.

I've been blessed with four beautiful children. Each one has taught me more than they know and more than I could ever hope to teach them in return. As I watch them grow and face new challenges head-on, I understand that a small amount of what I have instilled in them goes through their minds as they navigate the world. My oldest son has taught me how to be a parent and that things that seem scary at first are often not as daunting as they appear on the surface. My daughter has taught me to use the tools I'm given creatively and not care so much about what society says I should be or what I should do. My middle son has taught me to be different, see the world differently, and communicate in various ways. And my youngest son, though only two months old, has taught me to expect the unexpected. In return, I have been able to share with them my own experiences in life as they have watched me complete degrees, earn promotions, and experience loss with poise and dignity. They have also been able to watch me fall flat on my face sometimes, which I honestly think has been tremendously more valuable to them than watching me excel in life.

We have friends throughout our lives who come to us at just the right time and some who leave later than they should have. I did not grow up with many steadfast friends, and it was not until adulthood that I honestly had a best friend. In my youth, I frequently had friends come and go, and I often felt lost in crowded rooms. As I've gotten older, I realize a lot of that was due to anxiety and a lack of comfort in expressing myself appropriately. Still, as a teen and young adult, it often would materialize as anger, acting out, and getting into trouble. I was a boy-crazy teen; I'm not afraid to admit it, even knowing my children will likely read this chapter. I often felt alone, and if I was given a chance to spend time with someone, I did not feel I had the opportunity to be picky about who that person was or what they were doing. Looking back, I realize that as embarrassed or ashamed as I could be of the things I have done in my past, it has allowed me to discover who I want to be as an adult.

Then there are the friends we have now as adults. I'm fortunate to have met soulmates who exist in the form of friends who would be here for me in an instant. Those who hear of something I accomplish cheer me on in a way I never knew others could. The "twin flames" that exist in my life who treat my children as their own and really do create a village of support around my family, making many of my accomplishments possible. Throughout all seasons of my life, both fair-weather and lifelong friends have each shaped me in one way or another. Of course, the best of them reaches deeper into my heart than those who have since left my life.

Mentorship has been a large part of my life, and I have been fortunate to have had several mentors in varying degrees during different phases of my life. My mentors helped me realize that I was more than what I ever thought I could be while pushing me to continually look ahead while understanding the wake of what was left behind me. My personal drive to be a mentor to others is a direct result of their impact on me and has created a ripple effect that spans out further than any of us are fully aware of.

So many others have helped me achieve my goals in life: aunts (a couple of very vocal ones who requested specific mentions in this chapter), uncles, siblings, cousins, teachers, co-workers, employers, and more. And many of them have had a substantial impact on me as an individual. While much of this chapter is an ode to those who have helped me along the way, I hope that my ability to recognize the sometimes-unlikely source of support and encouragement is out there in each of our lives.

We have those who bring us apparent reinforcement and praise and those who might do it more subtly. Each person we let into our lives can leave an impression, and it is up to us to interpret and use it as something beneficial or detrimental. In my opinion, this choice is what many come to know as grit. Because it *is* a choice. The choice to look at what life has given us as either positive or negative. The choice to move forward with grace or misery. And the choice to keep challenging ourselves because those around us deserve our best version of us. The choice is mine, and it can also be yours.

Amanda Schroeder was born and raised in southern Illinois. She is a wife and mother of four beautiful children who challenge her daily. She is also the Chief Financial Officer at GadellNet Consulting Services and co-owns a small accounting firm with her husband in the metro-east area.

She is a PhD candidate in Organizational Leadership at Concordia University in Chicago, Illinois. Amanda earned her bachelor's degree in accounting and a master's degree in business administration from Southern Illinois University at Carbondale and her associate's degree in fine arts from Lewis and Clark Community College.

Amanda grew up in a small farming community and still resides in the same town to this day. In fact, she can see the street she grew up on from her current backyard! She enjoys meeting new people and especially loves mentoring those who seek leadership in their personal and professional lives. She loves to bake, paint, and spend time with friends and family. She also enjoys spending time outdoors and watching her children grow. Though it happens less frequently now that they have four children, Amanda and her husband love to travel and hope to one day see the world.

Please scan the QR code to connect with this author.

Jenny Gabriel

There is More to the Image Factor

I was eleven years old when my mother suffered a massive stroke and an aneurysm, which left her in a coma and a fetal state, meaning she had to learn how to walk, talk, read, and write all over again. She was in the hospital an hour away from us for several months. It was a result of her image issues and something deeper rooted than anyone else knew. She had been taking multiple prescription weight loss drugs and other medications, filling them at multiple pharmacies. On that one fateful night, her body responded to years of medication overuse by simply closing down.

I was afraid of my mom when she came home because she wasn't my mom any longer. She didn't look like her, act like her. I was terrified, but mostly, I was afraid the same thing would happen to her again.

At the age of eleven, this was hugely impactful and traumatizing to me. I was there that night. I watched it happen. Did I know then the connection with what I was going to do with this experience and the work that I'm doing today? No, but I knew that I didn't want to see somebody else go through what I did. I still try to work through some of that trauma because I was young, and I saw it unfold. I experienced her health issues leading up to the event and that one fateful night as I watched her body rebel against the abuse.

She was 36 years old when that happened, and I lost her when she was 56 and I was 31, pregnant with my first child. When she had that stroke, the aging of her body internally escalated, which led to more severe health issues over those next twenty years. The root cause was never addressed. She continued to struggle with her image and other deep-rooted issues, but the problem was no one really knew it had continued.

When she passed, we found out that she was still taking over-the-counter weight loss pills. The need was never fixed, never cured. We found weight loss pills in drawers, hidden in different places in the house, and places where no one would have known even to look. Her image factor cost me to lose her. It was devastating to me, my siblings, my father, and our entire family. At that time, she didn't have someone like me who could have worked with her on the nutritional lifestyle side of health. She also needed therapy to work through the real struggle for her mental health.

I never learned the "why" behind my mother's reasons. Her "why" was something so deeply rooted. Unfortunately, it was never discussed in our family. It was the silent killer and something no one wanted to discuss because the pain from it was so raw. Do I wish I had dived deeper and asked the questions? Absolutely, but then I don't think I did, out of respect for not hurting others who already were struggling with the outcome.

Today, I wish I could have pulled the band-aid off and had the hard conversations. It might have helped all of us with healing and closure. I lost my dad suddenly seven years ago, so the hopes of that happening have been lost. I wish that ship hadn't already sailed. There just weren't answers. It wasn't that someone was necessarily holding them back, either. It was how my family dealt with the situation.

Honestly, talking about this, writing this chapter, and helping clients explore their process is my journey in closure and healing.

My quest and what I do as a nutritional therapy practitioner is to offer women the understanding that there is more to this image factor. Especially through the menopausal years, there is support. I have found that when women go to the physician's office for help, they're not getting what they need. They are being told, "That's just how it is, or take this for this," without guidance or understanding of what lies at the root cause of the symptoms they are experiencing.

Medical intervention also needs to be a part of the treatment plan. But there's also another side that I feel like women need to realize. There are natural ways of facing and treating what's going on, which gives women the opportunity to utilize more holistic therapies in their menopausal journey.

My quest is to help other women.

We have been led to believe and are surrounded by messages everywhere that we need to look, feel, and act in a certain way. There is a lot of static, and it is due time to filter through it all.

My quest in life is working with women 35 to 65 years old.

There are strategies I can offer that will help women live a vibrant, healthy life. We are seeing staggering health statistics about women in these menopausal years, including an increase in suicide due to hormonal shifts, metabolic health, and all the outside static that's happening in our world. With this image pressure, we're also seeing women resorting to strategies without thinking through the long-term health effects, such as weight loss injections and drugs. Many women do not need to use weight loss drugs, especially if they are not aware of their whole health picture. In circumstances where this is warranted, a trusted medical provider is imperative, along with a nutrition practitioner, to address lifestyle changes.

My quest is to help women understand and realize how to live a long life with lifestyle changes, including how to handle stress, sleep management, and the ability to navigate special events with family and friends without feeling restricted in their food choices.

When I work with clients, I teach them how to look at food differently, shift their mindset, include a movement piece, and look at possible supplements—understanding what supplementation can do, not the promises that it will fix everything. The reality is that if it is too good to be true, it likely is!

We live in a society now where we are depleted of many vitamins and minerals due to toxins in the air, products, cooking utensils, foods, and the quality of foods. Sometimes, proper supplementation is necessary. Within my practice, I make sure clients have practitioner-grade supplements that have been tested for quality, bacterial pathogens, and heavy metals. With supplementation, there can be cross contamination. I need to make sure a client knows what is flaring.

I work with clients on a cellular level, and all the work I do is based on science. I take a holistic approach from inside to outside. Testing is completed by using hair tissue manual analysis, which is called HTMA; it looks at our cells over the last ninety days, and it can give me a clear picture, cellularly, of what's going on inside the female body. I primarily work with women, but the testing works on a male body as well. This allows us to get a good grasp of where things are, such as mineral and vitamin status. This can explain some of the symptoms clients are having.

A nutritional assessment questionnaire gives me more insight, including what a client's current lifestyle and diet look like. This is one of my favorite tools to evaluate dietary habits, overall health, and nutritional status of my clients. It gathers information on eating patterns, lifestyle choices, and medical history to identify potential nutritional deficiencies or excess, including GI, adrenal, blood sugar handling, liver, kidney, gallbladder, and female health. The data I gather from the testing helps me personalize and tailor precise dietary recommendations, lifestyle suggestions, and a supplementation plan for each client, which addresses their unique health and wellness concerns.

I also use metabolic flexibility and can tell if someone is staying stuck in a sugar-burning state, unable to go back and forth between fat burning and sugar burning. I see that too often with women in this age group because of their prior diet or chemicals in our current food supply. This sometimes makes us become more insulin resistant instead of insulin sensitive. We also work on decreasing toxins. We work on the things that they're willing to try to remove because that will help open their detoxification pathways. Sometimes, this gets restricted and backed up, not actually letting those toxins flow like they should.

There is a lot of outside static in our world and daily lives, and I talk to my clients about this and how to clear it. Internal stress prevents us from detoxing, as well as the stress of scrolling, which can be damaging. We're constantly subconsciously comparing ourselves to others on that screen, looking for the next best cure, the next best answer, the next best "fill in the blank." How can I be this person or this image society has created for us to be? It becomes very confusing and stressful at the same time. While we're doing that, our eye movement is up and down, causing our cortisol levels to spike. It signals the nervous system in the body that there's a bear or tiger chasing them. The nervous system can get frozen in that state if we do this too much.

Another strategy I use with clients is recording our conversations as a follow-up, which includes bullet points and direct links to our conversation. Brain fog is a real thing for menopausal women. How many of us don't remember why we went in the other room or where we put our glasses, and they're on top of our head where we put them? I also suggest my clients buy a binder for resources, notes, and protocols we've discussed. This allows them to have all the tools in their toolbox when they fly on their own.

There is another strategy I find important. If I have a client that needs additional help with mental health, I have a referral list for therapy and other services. With a gentle suggestion, I can say, "You need to go here for therapy to work on that part. We'll work on this part together here." I implement this because I think if my mom would have had me or a professional like me, then we could have put a support plan together for her. Help that would have offered my mom the support and direction she needed to see that there was more to getting and feeling healthy. And it wasn't just about image.

Many women come to me with image/weight as their top concern. After our work together they understand that their concerns were really about overall health, and they leave with the best possible plan for optimal longevity.

At the end of the day, we are beautiful in the temple God gave us. Living a well-rounded wellness journey is what I want women to know is most important. It is taking small, healthy steps to add years to our life. It is about healthy lifestyle choices now that will help us feel how we want to in our 60s, 70s, 80s, and beyond.

My quest and what I do as a nutritional therapy practitioner is to offer women the understanding that there is more to this image factor. My quest is to offer strategies that help women live a vibrant, healthy life. It is my tribute to my mom.

Jenny Gabriel, MAOM, NTP, HMTA-P, FLAG, FSS, CPT, is the owner of JG Optimal Wellness and is a nutritional therapy practitioner located in Wentzville, MO.

Her journey in the field of health and well-being has been guided by a deep passion for helping women going through the menopausal transition at any stage achieve optimal health and vitality.

Jenny is a member of the Creve Coeur-Olivette Chamber, G.R.I.T., Little Black Book, and various women's networking groups. She has been a featured speaker educating on women's health and wellness during meno"pause."

Jenny is a dedicated mother, loves to read for leisure, enjoys being outdoors with exercise, and enjoys spending time with her husband, two college-age boys, and their fur baby, Brenlee.

Please scan the QR code to connect with this author.

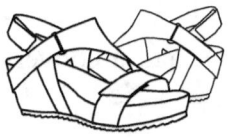

Marsha Russo

Hardship to Happiness

"But until a person can say deeply and honestly, 'I am what I am today because of the choices I made yesterday,' that person cannot say, 'I choose otherwise.'" – Stephen R. Covey

In a world full of endless ups and downs, I can confidently say that without every struggle, heartache, and challenge, I would not be who I am today. Without making a conscious choice to fight for myself, my boys, and the type of relationship I wanted, my life could look vastly different. There was a little luck and a higher power at play to help me maneuver this crazy life journey, but every day is a blessing, and I'm so lucky to live it with a wonderful man who appreciates me and how we both got here together.

My husband, Tony, and I met when I was only fifteen and he was nineteen. That is how the story began, but far from how we got to where we are today. At fifteen, I was not allowed to date a nineteen-year-old, so it was solely chance that we met at an ice skating rink over summer break. I didn't know how to ice skate, so he would hold my hand and help me skate. At the end of summer, that was it. We never kissed and didn't call one another; it was just a random occurrence in our lives. Over the years, we ran into one another a couple of times, but we never muttered more than "Hi, how's it going?" Fourteen years later, after getting divorced and having two children, I ran into him again, but this time, we were both older and wiser. We stopped, had a conversation, exchanged numbers, and nearly a year later, we were married.

Life is bigger than we think. Every occurrence leads to next steps. Whether good, bad, or melancholy, every action, reaction, and chance circumstance leads us somewhere. While I'd love to say it would be great to reverse all the bad things that happened along the way, that would mean erasing many life lessons that have shaped my life today and the blessings that came along with learning from those hardships.

From an early age I was a dreamer, had grand ideas, lofty goals, loved adventure, and was fiercely independent. At seventeen, I graduated high school and moved to Florida. I was simply seeking adventure and freedom, choosing not to attend college. It was great learning experience working two jobs, renting my own apartment, buying my first car, and learning how to manage money and live on my own. Driving eighteen hours from St. Louis to Florida alone at that age with only a map and no GPS or cell phone back then was crazy.

Two years into my Florida experience, one of the girls who had become a close friend was murdered. That was enough of a shock and wake-up call for me to come back to St. Louis. Those two years taught me how much I missed and enjoyed time with family. Losing my friend was a harsh reminder that life is short and we can't take anything for granted. That period of my life gave me a new perspective and a sense of respect for my parents, who worked hard to ensure we had food, education, financial security, and love while still giving us the latitude to make decisions that were sometimes wrong so we could learn from our mistakes and grow in the process.

Once back in St. Louis, I enrolled in school and took a job in a restaurant to pay my way. My life took a turn at this junction, dating a guy from work who was quite a bit older. He was divorced, edgy, and intriguing.

Our dating became serious much too quickly. I found myself engaged by the time I was twenty-one and married by twenty-two. Our relationship was tumultuous. He was argumentative and continually found ways to belittle me while slowly chipping away at my confidence and self-worth. He regularly referred to me as "stupid" or an "idiot," and while the abuse was primarily mental, he would occasionally get mildly physical to further intimidate me. I thought I was doing something wrong, so I bought books and tapes to figure out how to be a better wife and improve our relationship. That adventurous, independent girl was gone, and I felt as though I didn't know who I was anymore.

At the time, I felt divorce was not an option. I did not want to fail or be perceived by others as a failure. Over the six years we were married, we had two children. The verbal abuse worsened, and then there was infidelity. I reached a breaking point and couldn't fathom living a miserable life and allowing my children to see how I was mistreated. It was so important to me that my boys understood that women should be treated with respect and that relationships were about unconditional love, communication, and understanding.

The life we were living did not represent my beliefs and was in no way a representation of how I was raised. When my boys were three months and three years old, I decided it was enough. I filed a restraining order, giving me approximately two weeks to find a house, move out, and start over. I sold my wedding ring and tennis bracelet to use for a down payment on a cute little ranch spec home in a new construction subdivision. On December 16, 1998, my boys and I moved into our new home.

Leaving that relationship was the best decision I ever made. My boys and I celebrated by having a slumber party. We slept in sleeping bags on the floor, made popcorn, danced, and watched movies. It was a new beginning, and we were on our way to making new *happy* memories.

Here is where magic happens. My husband and I ran into each other a few months after my marriage ended. We talked about how we had met fourteen years prior and what a strange twist of fate that we met again after we had both undergone so many struggles. I'm confident God planted a seed allowing us to meet when we were younger, and when we had both matured and experienced the necessary life lessons, we were able to come together with a renewed sense of understanding, empathy, and encouragement for one another. He was kind to me, which really resonated as I don't know that I would have appreciated that kindness, having been deprived of it for so long in a loveless and abusive marriage. It's just something that feels so important to our story, and I love how we got here.

My ex moved out of town when my boys were two and five years old, and my husband, Tony, adopted my boys a year after we were married. He has been the father and husband we needed and deserved. I'm so thankful for all the twists and turns we took on our journey. It's been over twenty-four years, and we just get stronger each year, surviving teenagers, job losses, financial struggles, and much more. We never give up, are always committed to one another, and wouldn't be who we are today without all the hardships, obstacles, mistakes, and lessons learned over the years.

It was out of hardship that we made the decision to start our first business, Russo Stone Design. The economic meltdown in 2007 and 2008 left us without jobs; both of our industries were severely impacted, and we couldn't find employment. Fortunately, we had money set aside for our kids' college that we used to survive during that difficult time. We downsized our home, pulled our kids out of private school, canceled memberships, and cashed in our last 401k to start the business. Seventeen years later, Tony has continued to support our family with his tenacity to grow that business into a well-respected name in the St. Louis market.

At the time of the economic meltdown, I had been in wholesale lending and eventually was able to secure a role with a startup company helping grow their brand in the St. Louis market. I continued working in the lending arena over the years, helping new companies grow their footprint, and I was able to make a good living. In 2019, I took a hiatus from the lending space and accepted a sales position for a home warranty company launching in our market. I loved the idea of building something from nothing.

My first year in this role, we found ourselves in the middle of a pandemic, unable to network and sponsor events. Seeking a new way to connect, I reached out to people on Facebook and began sharing fitness tips and scheduling "walk and talk" meetings either in person or virtually. This gave me a platform to get to know people one-to-one and build relationships. My business grew during this experiment; people became familiar with who I was and subsequently started using my home warranty product. I received the Gold Star Award that year and was nominated for Rookie of the Year solely because I decided to try something new. I met some of my closest friends during those two years working for the home warranty industry, even though I never actually enjoyed selling home warranties and ultimately went back to lending.

In 2021, I was asked to bring a new wholesale company to market with a team I had worked with previously. It was one of the best experiences of my career, working with an all-star team of individuals. We were building something extremely special with this new wholesale platform. In less than two years, we had already grown to be a top ten wholesale lender in the country. Then the market turned, and our business took a nosedive. After several rounds of layoffs, corporate decided to pull funding on the project and shut down the wholesale platform.

So here we go again, losing my job. It was at this time that my mom got sick and ended up in the hospital for more than a month. In the end, she lost her battle due to numerous complications. Losing her was another turning point for me. She had been a focal point in my life for several years, giving me a sense of purpose. I drove her to doctor appointments, took her dog to the vet, and spent a day or two each week working from her home and spending time with her. Losing her shortly after losing my job was a low point. I needed a fresh start in something completely new and different.

I began working with a business coach to help find a direction and look at franchise options. After researching several companies, we decided to do something we could assimilate with our other business. It was important for me to bring a new brand to market as that was the environment where I thrived in the past. We are now a little over a year into Bumble Bee Blinds as a business. It has been hard and a learning experience, but it's just another example of how life keeps setting us in the right place at the right time. Between our relationships made over the years with designers, custom builders, and remodelers with Russo Stone to the numerous relationships I made during the pandemic working in home warranty, and relationships made during my tenured lending career, it proves there is a greater purpose behind everything we do in our lives.

In the end, there are so many things that shape the trajectory of our lives. Failure is part of succeeding, mistakes provide valuable lessons, and hardship tests our resilience and will only make us stronger. Keep choosing to move forward, strive to achieve your goals, take the occasional risk, and find the silver lining. I can promise you that no matter the circumstance, there is always a message in the madness, and magic happens when you least expect it.

"The greatest glory in living lies not in never failing,
but in rising every time we fail."
-Nelson Mandela

Marsha spent over twenty-five years in wholesale lending, assisting new companies transitioning from brand anonymity to well-established identities nationwide. During her tenure as a top producer, she aided in the exponential growth of new platforms and was chosen to speak to over a thousand businesswomen about building value and fast-tracking their careers at the National Women's Leadership Annual Summit. She's now embarked on her own journey to entrepreneurship, opening Bumble Bee Blinds in 2023. She's championed by her husband, Tony, who is also an entrepreneur, opening Russo Stone Design in 2008. Married for twenty-four years, they have two adult children, Ryan and Jarrod Russo, and two fur babies, Bash and Bosco. Tony and Marsha relish exploring small towns around the United States as well as the local restaurant scene. Marsha loves spending time with family and friends, thrives on adventure, and enjoys all things fitness.

Please scan the QR code to connect with this author.

Ali Carson

Hidden Lessons

I'm a small-town girl who had the fortune to be raised by some pretty amazing parents. Now, by amazing, I don't mean they found cures for diseases or were rich or famous. Quite the contrary, in fact. My parents, Jack and Beccy, were a farmer and a teacher, but amazing, nonetheless. You see, this farmer, Jack, was the youngest person ever elected to serve as mayor of my hometown. He also served on the county board and various agricultural initiatives. And this teacher, Beccy, went on to become an administrator. As an elementary school principal, my mom implemented a weekly late start in her small rural school district focused on teacher professional development. This was in the 90s when that just wasn't done. She led that small school district to recognition by the state for innovation in professional development, a path that she would continue for the rest of her career.

I believe what helped them achieve such success came from foundational beliefs they held which they passed on to my sisters and I in the form of "isms."

"Isms" are those catchy phrases someone says so frequently it becomes what they are known for. My parents had lots of "isms." I'm a words person, so I collected those phrases like some people collect souvenirs. What I've come to know as an adult was that these phrases weren't just kooky things my parents said. Within them were hidden lessons that served to shape me. My work ethic, my persistence, my grit—all can be traced back to these kitschy phrases I heard over and over from my mom and dad. They had many "isms" but I'm going share a few of my favorites with you. Five favorites to be exact—each with a lesson that you can apply in both your professional and personal lives.

Number 1: We're burnin' daylight.

Picture a man with a big cowboy hat, mustache, and an ornery grin—that's my dad. That wasn't a phase or a fashion statement. That was who he was—cowboy through and through from his boots to the tip of his 10-gallon hat. One of the "isms" we heard from him so often growing up (and honestly well after we'd all grown up and moved away) was "We're burnin' daylight!" Growing up this often happened when Dad was trying to get us out the door to get somewhere—which I'm sure you can imagine with four daughters didn't always happen in a timely fashion. But he also used it anytime we needed a boost to get moving. The hidden lesson in this "ism" was to get up, get going, and get something done.

How many times in your professional life have you talked about a problem… and talked… and talked… and talked. If you're like most people I know, at one point or another you have talked up and down around that problem without getting one step closer to solving it. You hit that analysis paralysis and can't seem to make the move to action. Now, when I find myself in these moments, I'll simply say, "We're burnin' daylight." This has become my procrastination cure, my mantra for movement. And it's amazing how effective it is. Get up. Get going. Get something done. We're burnin' daylight.

Number 2: You're always interviewing for your next job.

This one is from my mom. She was an educator, and a damn good one at that. As an educator, she dressed up for work every day. Even when she was running a pre-school from the basement in our home, she dressed for the part. Why? Because she knew her appearance would leave an impression—whether she meant to or not—and wanted it to be a favorable one. I can remember mom making us dress up for church when other families were arriving in jeans (again, back in the 90s when this wasn't as common as it is today). Or making us dress up for school events when our friends weren't. It drove me crazy that I couldn't just be comfy like my friends, that I had to dress up when others weren't. And when I would bemoan that fact, she'd just get a little smile on her face and tell me it was because "you're always interviewing for your next job."

But of course, she knew something we didn't. She knew that every interaction we have with someone is an opportunity to make an impression, good, bad, or otherwise. And she knew that you never know when those opportunities may arrive to make a good impression. You want to be prepared. She knew that the way you present yourself to the world—not only with your clothes but with your presence, your confidence—could help you make an impression that may one day open a door to an opportunity you can't even see right now. Because you're always interviewing for your next job.

Number 3: Dress for the job you want, not the job you have.

This is another Beccy-ism. When mom was dressing up to teach preschool in our basement, she wasn't really trying to impress a bunch of four-year olds. She was dressing for the job she knew she may want to return to—being a classroom teacher in a school. In my twenty years working in the corporate world, I held at least fourteen different roles, yet I only applied and interviewed for five of them. One third. The other two thirds of the roles I earned happened because someone saw the potential in me to contribute in bigger and better ways because of how I showed up every day. I've always been motivated and had high aspirations. I can also get a bit bored when the work stops being a challenge. As soon as I mastered the work in one role, I started asking for stretch assignments and opportunities to do things that may not be part of my actual job description. What that showed was being a fast learner with determination and initiative that made it easy for all those different leaders to promote me.

The hidden lesson here is about your mental preparation and thinking ahead. If you are already working at the next level in your current role, you are thinking about the work differently. You solve problems differently. You show up differently. And sometimes, you dress differently. You put on the mindset of someone who has the job you want, and then you start acting like someone who has the job you want. This not only increases your confidence, but it also increases others' confidence in your competence. Which ultimately helps you get that next job. So, dress for the job you want, not the job you have.

Number 4: It puts hair on your chest.

As I'm sure you can imagine, this one did *not* come from the teacher. In fact, it would often earn dad one of mom's famous "10-pound teacher frowns" whenever he said it. This one came from the cowboy, and I not only remember him saying it to my sisters and I, but later to our kids. In fact, I can vividly recall when my son Colt was about four years old. We were visiting my parents and having breakfast. If you've ever had a four-year-old or been around one, you may know that their preferences can change in an instant. One day their favorite food is macaroni and cheese, the next day it's the worst food on the planet. At this breakfast, Colt had apparently had a shift in his preferences and no longer liked the blueberries he had devoured the day before. As Grandpa was trying to cajole him into eating them, he said, "Go on. Eat 'em up! They'll put hair on your chest!" To which my ornery four-year-old replied, "Well you must have eaten *a lot* of them!" I think in that instance my dad's words may have had the opposite effect to what he had intended.

This one took me longer to find the hidden lesson. What I finally figured out was that when you realized something scared you or it wasn't something you wanted to do, it was okay to be brave enough to do it anyway. In being brave, you become braver. We've heard this in all sorts of phrases from authors over the years—eat the frog, take the leap, dive into the deep end. What is the one thing that you would love to do, that you wake up thinking about, that energizes you every single time—but you hesitate to take the leap? What's holding you back? Ask yourself this, will I regret *not* doing this a year from now? And if the answer is yes, do it. Go ahead—it'll put hair on your chest!

Number 5: Be smarter than the rest of the turkeys.

Every time my sisters or I left the house, my mom would ask the usual questions—Where were we going? Who were we going with? When would we be home? Once those questions were answered to her satisfaction, we were cleared to take off. But before we got out the door, she would always say, "Be smarter than the rest of the turkeys." It was her way of telling us to be safe, make good choices, and help our friends make good choices as well. I studied abroad and lived in London for a semester in college. Looking back now with a seventeen-year-old, adventure-seeking daughter of my own, I can only imagine the fears that ran through her head when she sent her then twenty-year-old to another country for three months! That was when this "ism" got updated—she'd tell me to "Be smarter than the rest of the turkeys, and watch out for the fox!" I think she thought some of the cute boys with accents I told her about in our weekly phone calls may have had some sneaky intentions.

The hidden lesson in this one is all about who we choose to surround ourselves with. We know, and research has shown, that we are heavily influenced by the company we keep—the people we spend the most time with. And it's not just face to face time—it's also who is on our social media feed, the tv and movies we watch, the list goes on. My question to you is this—is the company you keep lifting you up, or bringing you down? Is your social media feed filled with people who make you feel better after you read their content? Or do you feel the drain of comparison and insecurity dragging you down? We each have the opportunity to curate our world—to an extent. By curating I mean hand-picking with intention. We can do that in almost every aspect of our lives. Who do we eat lunch with at work? Who do we spend our time with on the weekends? Who do we follow on social media? We want to surround ourselves with uplifting people and messages who help us be stronger, more resilient, more effective. So be smarter than the rest of the turkeys, and watch out for the fox!

In 2021, we lost my father after a 10-year battle with brain tumors. In 2023, my mother passed away unexpectedly. The past three years were some of the hardest of my life with many lessons of their own. I've learned that grief is a sneaky b*tch who likes to come in when you least expect her to steal your breath and break your heart all over again. But I've also learned that the lessons from my parents stay with me and in many ways prepared me with the grit I would ultimately tap into to survive these tremendous losses. I want to share these lessons with the world so that their legacy and the impact they had on so many can continue. I know my parents are proud of all four of their daughters—for the women we've become, for the way we've handled these loses, and for learning how to live well with grit.

Ali Carson is an experienced coach and dynamic facilitator with two decades of experience working in all aspects of human resources, learning, and development.

Ali is the founder and CEO of Movere Coaching, LLC, where she works with high-achieving professionals, leaders, and teams to achieve greater results through coaching, leadership development, and team effectiveness solutions.

She is passionate about creating workplaces where everyone can thrive. Prior to founding Movere Coaching, Ali served as a senior leader in talent development for an Am200 law firm. Her prior experience also includes progressive leadership roles in learning and organizational development for a large, non-profit health care system.

Ali holds several professional certifications, showcasing her dedication to excellence. As a Gallup-Certified Strengths Coach, she specializes in helping clients discover and maximize their strengths.

Ali is also a Results-Certified Brain-Based Coach, bringing tools founded in neuroscience to her strengths-based approach to create impactful coaching and learning experiences for her clients.

Please scan the QR code to connect with this author.

Denise Hedrick Huber

Smiling Through the Hard Stuff

The meaning of my life lived well is to find my gift, and the purpose of my life lived well is to give it away with grit. I found my gift early in life. God smiled on me enthusiastically to persevere in Gratitude, Resilience, Intention, and Tenacity, especially through the hard stuff.

The experience of hard stuff in my life challenged me. Though humbled, I was empowered to understand who I am, whose I am, and who I serve. Finding my *Living Well* gift early in life has been a blessing. The rest of my life would be spent seeking wisdom and serving others.

You may relate to the statement, "Life is messy." My first eight years of life were messy, but I found my gift! This wisdom enlightened us to be a family team with dreams. Our plan focused on encouraging each other to seek good words, good thoughts, and good deeds. My story is full of *living well with grit*, challenges, and seeking the light in dark choices. It makes me smile, and I am joyful to begin with the two people who made it all happen.

My parents were high school sweethearts and dated through college. My mother graduated first with a nursing degree from St. Johns Mercy Hospital/St. Louis University. She took her first assignment at the Veterans Hospital in Rolla, Missouri, to be close to my father. He graduated from

Missouri S&T with an engineering degree, and they got married that same summer. Within a few months as newlyweds, they discovered they were pregnant with me, and the family team began to create the dream.

While working in the hospital, she's informed she's been exposed to German measles. Given the risks, she was told to consider options for her unborn child. They placed their trust and faith in God and continued the pregnancy. Fortuitously, my dad accepts an engineering job and they move to a new home in Toledo, Ohio. Once they settle into their new location, they decide my mother will stay home and prepare for their first baby.

Her pregnancy remained uneventful, and the moment I was born, my parents smiled with gratitude. I was born a healthy, brown-eyed, brown-haired, two-legs and two-arms baby girl. My arrival relieved many thoughts for my parents. Fortunately, they had leaned into their faith. They smiled through this hard time and created a foundation seeking gratitude, resilience, good intentions, and tenacity. They strengthened their trust in God and were blessed with a smiling, bright-eyed Denise Ann Hedrick. This encouraged their belief that God would make all things work for good when they said yes to life.

Our small family operated around my enthusiastic energy in my first months! This gave them confidence that I was definitely well. I zipped through crawling and onto walking at a young six months of age. This impressed the doctors and nurses, and I became wise to the energy that connected me to others. I learned smiling, and people smiling back at me, was a good way to make friends.

When I was two, my parents openly welcomed another healthy baby girl. She was a delightful gift and different from me. She had beautiful strawberry-blonde hair, blue eyes, and a gentle personality. Our similarity was our smiles. And I loved the way my enthusiasm made her happy, whether my sister liked it or not.

I was a lot to handle, which made it challenging to implement a family plan. When I turned three and my sister was one, my parents decided it was time for my mom to take a night nursing assignment at the Toledo Hospital. They secured childcare, and like many children, I struggled to acclimate to a new schedule and care plan. My biggest downfall was my resistance to rest and nap, and it became a problem. They consider many reasons why, when suddenly, all I want to do is rest and nap, and my smile is missing. This behavior alarms my mother, and she knows something is very wrong.

I had a 104-degree fever, and my parents took me to the hospital, where my mother had just started her nursing assignment. The irony of me at my mother's workplace would be considered a life-giving smile through this hard time. I stayed there for the next six weeks, overcoming a life-threatening illness. My health discovery took many turns, especially when my mother heard that the top Cleveland Clinic pediatric oncologist was visiting my case. This specialist would rule out leukemia and recommend another path to wellness. It was a very hard time for my family. And I learned to seek warm, loving smiles from those who visited me. Even when the news and treatments were not good, the doctors and nurses gave me smiles. This would give me the hope and energy to persevere. God instilled a smile in my heart as I endured the hospitalization and health challenges.

Gratefully, while I was secured at the hospital, my parents were loved by their neighbors, friends, and faith community. This helped my parents restore each night and have the energy to love and care for my sister. This also allowed my parents to be at every possible visiting hour. I am confident that God smiled on me with my guardian angel at my side, especially when I was secured in bed to administer treatments, medicine, and rest. At last, I am diagnosed with an autoimmune disease, Juvenile Rheumatoid

Arthritis, and I receive a new life wellness plan. This is when a smile really made a difference through medicine, treatments, and arthritic pain. The difference in me before the hospital and after the hospital was striking. And gratefully, I went from boundless enthusiastic energy to a little three-year-old self who was lethargic, puffy from steroids, and ached. I didn't understand it, but I loved the hope I received to live better.

We found encouragement from many sources to live well. We moved forward with our new wellness normal. As our family continued enjoying life, we got the good news that we would welcome a new sibling. My parents decided to accept my dad's job promotion, and we packed up our lives to relocate. We secured our living well plan and medical records and moved to a new home. My mother's pregnancy is considered uneventful and there is a lot of hope. Our brother is born within a few months of moving to Marshalltown, Iowa. I am almost five years old and very excited to welcome him. However, this begins a whole new level of difficulty. And our smiles are not prepared for this next challenge.

His arrival is unexpectedly messy. He was born with his spinal cord frayed and uncontained. He was whisked away to a critical care hospital two hours away from our town. His emergency needs were profound. He is diagnosed with spina bifida and paralysis. And yet, it was his smile that made caring for him a joy. Thank God for our optimistic, family-team attitude, along with our large team of healthcare professionals, all desiring my brother's wellness because they honored our desire to care for his life. Our family was considered unique because we wanted to bring him home for care.

My parents modeled tenacity and committed to doing whatever it took to make his life well and our home able to accommodate his needs. My sister and I were enthusiastically on board and leaned into our care roles. Led by compassion, we were willing to be his hands and feet. Led by our parents' intentions, our home became a training ground for administering home therapy to a special child with complex needs. We followed their lead joyfully because we all found smiles in the new family normal. We found inspiration to endure this new life challenge—together.

I continued healing with my JRA regimen, and the spirit filled us. My symptoms persisted but were minimal in comparison to my brother's needs. It was hard, messy work. However, we were surrounded by lots of love from others. We could not have done this new normal without our Marshalltown, Iowa, community. They were special, and we were blessed. We felt God smiling on us.

We had an operational wellness plan and help at every turn. Our friends supported our family team, filling us with dreams and hopes, including helping our brother eventually stand up on his paralyzed legs with brace support. It was glorious news, and then we got more good news. Our family team would welcome another sibling. We received the news when my brother was three, my sister was five, and I was seven. Her arrival warmed our hearts, especially since she was born on a cold northern blizzard day and on St. Nicholas Day. She was healthy, with blue eyes and blond hair, and we brought her home to join our dream team. And, of course, we named this Advent blessing Nicole.

Her precious baby ways made us smile, especially through the hard stuff of our lives. My dad made an intentional habit of documenting our lives with pictures and videos. This was a profound gift to remember our family life's memories. And I am incredibly grateful to my parents for living a life full of activities. All of the activities created energy and connected us to others. And thank God because the next breathtaking, messy moments happen, and our smiles are wiped off our faces.

My brother's health took a deathly turn. He tragically passed onto heaven because of health complications. In his four short years here on earth, he taught us wisdom. His life empowered us. Our brother was considered "a smile that God built a boy around," and now his smile was gone. I'm sure you can understand that we were heartbroken and did not find smiling easy. However, we still had a baby girl to help her instill that precious delight in life. We also had each other to put smiles back on our faces even when we did not feel like smiling. Her little joys kept us focused on living.

God rooted our foundation in faith and trust in God's providence. Our greatest challenge in life would be how to live with the emptiness we all felt with our brother's smile passing from us. We thought we knew how to do life well, and we learned unconditional love from our little angel brother. And without him, smiling and breathing became extremely hard.

Many years have passed since we last saw his smile. Now that I've had the chance to reflect on how I found my gift of living well with my smile, I can see clearly that my brother's life was a gift. It is his inspiration from God and our family that I now spend my life giving away this gift of my smile.

I know my family trusted in God, and I love this way. My family's life was "messy" and hard. Hopefully, you can see how my smile endured through these hard times, and it will allow you to find gratitude in your own life's messiness. Through this journey, I found purpose in giving away my smile to elevate others, including establishing a foundation in family care services at Martha's Hands. I pray we all continue to seek blessings in good words, good thoughts, and good deeds; and always with the gift of a smile.

Denise Hedrick Huber has been married for 34 years and is the joyful mother of six children. A lifelong entrepreneur, Denise is the co-founder and inspirational leader of her 250-member team at Martha's Hands Home Care and Wellness. An industry leader since 1997, Martha's Hands has provided over six million hours of care in the homes of older adults.

The foundations of Denise's chapter on living well are rooted in her small-town experiences growing up in Ohio and Iowa. Through the tough life challenges during that period, Denise established her grit through a strong faith, a sense of service, and a smile.

Please scan the QR code to connect with this author.

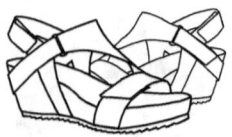

Julie Kappen

Finding Strength in Struggle

To start, I would like to preface by stating that living well is an ongoing work in progress for me. I do not pretend to have a secret to living well or any one concept for doing so or that it is mastered every day. Additionally, living well can mean very different things to different people. Maybe it is financial stability, mental or physical well-being, or simply a state of mind for some. For me, it is a wide array of components in my life that contribute to what I would consider living well. And that can fluctuate from day to day.

My life's journey has helped shape who I am today. Like everyone, I have evolved as I have grown and aged. Who I was 10, 15, or 20 years ago is not the person that I am today. Heck, I am not the same person I was before the pandemic, but I believe that event changed everyone in some form or fashion.

When I was young and growing up in a middle-class home in a rural community with three siblings and two very loving parents, we were taught that a strong work ethic can take you far. And for me, it has, but my path did not come without its own challenges.

Medical conditions during my young, formative years, which often came with pain and some humiliation, shaped who I have become and how I live my life.

Starting in grade school, during a standard spinal check, it was determined that I had scoliosis. Once I hit puberty in middle school, the scoliosis continued to worsen. As a result, I was required to wear a back brace, from chest to pelvis, for 23 hours a day, seven days a week through both seventh and eighth grade; mortifying, I know. That was one of my first defining moments, where I could choose to feel sorry for myself and hide or be brave. I decided to laugh it off and embrace this new "body armor," or as my family and I liked to call it, my "turtle shell."

Thankfully, it was under my clothes, so most of the kids in school likely did not know I even wore it, but since it was hard plastic, when I bent over, it would poke out. As a middle school kid, it felt like the entire world knew that I was wearing this contraption. To embrace and overcome it, I would tell the kids in school that I did abdominal exercises and my abs were rock solid, even asking them to punch me in the gut, only for their fists to be met with hard plastic. I decided this constrictive device was not going to control my life.

When I was 15 years old, I had my first grand mal seizure while staying at a friend's home. I was diagnosed with epilepsy and put on medication, which, when taken as prescribed, would prevent seizures from occurring. Thankfully, this condition was easily treatable with medication. While I did have a second seizure during a class in high school and a third as an adult, it was not something I could control, and therefore, I did not let it control me.

Fast forward to post-high school, and I am told that the brace I wore for scoliosis, while it held the curvature in my spine during my puberty growth phase, the curve was not going to stop progressing. At age 20, I had to decide if I wanted to have spinal fusion surgery or wait until I was older, as the back pain that I had been experiencing would only get worse. Understanding that it would be easier to recover and heal from a major surgery like this while I was young, I decided to have the six-hour surgery, where metal rods and screws were placed along my spine to correct the curve and prevent further curvature. I was hospitalized for an entire week, and it was a few months before I could return to work. This may seem like a lot for a young person to experience, but my health journey did not end there.

By age 21, I was diagnosed with an autoimmune disease that was impacting my weight and causing severe anemia. This condition brought significant challenges before, during, and after the pregnancy of my only child, including a very complex, two-part surgery by the age of 28. It continues to impact my daily life and will for the rest of my days.

When I think about living well, these conditions were the catalyst for being mindful of my physical and mental well-being. However, it did not start this way; there has been a lot of trial and error and learning the hard way to get to where I am today, decades later.

I have had to learn to be my own health advocate and push against the traditional Western medicine protocols, sometimes successfully and sometimes not. Finding alternative avenues, physicians, etc., has become commonplace for me. I am continuously working on my mental well-being as it can very easily slip into a victim mentality or the feeling that it is too hard to live a life of constant awareness and health struggles.

Living well in my late 40s looks very different than it did when I was younger. Today, it is not only comprised of physical and mental wellness but also pertains to the work that I do and the relationships that I have in my life. These impact our lives for better or worse. Is the work, either my job or voluntary, that I am doing satisfying? Do I feel like I am bringing value to those that I serve? Am I being fulfilled?

I am much more conscious about who I surround myself with now. Do those around me bring joy or drama? Are they taking more than they are giving? How do I feel about myself when I am with them? These are things that I ask myself periodically. There are times that I have had to adjust to both work and social aspects. These are never easy decisions, and I have gotten it wrong at times, but this is how we learn and truly live well in our lives.

Another area of my life that I believe reflects living well is around personal and professional growth. Something many are surprised to learn about me is that I do not have a college degree. It is not something that I am particularly proud of, but after attending community college following high school, I understood early that it was not a path that I wanted to pursue. I was working as a retail supervisor by the time I was a senior in high school on a work-study program. I was responsible for opening and closing the store and supervising those on the shift at the age of 17.

With hard work and a tenacity to learn and understand anything that anyone would train or teach me, I was able to progress at the organizations that I worked within throughout my career. There have been many times that I have been reluctant to contribute to conversations about college life experiences with colleagues out of embarrassment or shame. However, the older I get and the more successful I have become in my career, I have realized that I have been able to achieve the same level as most, and in many cases, more than my peers who did obtain a college degree. Do not get me wrong, I believe that education is very important and commend those who worked hard to obtain any level of advanced education. I am proud of my accomplishments that came from my hard work and effort. While I did not seek higher education, I have always continued to learn and absorb anything that I can through reading and attending webinars and training sessions, or courses that can bring information or value to me and my growth.

One additional area that I believe is critical is giving back to others. When you are blessed to either be born into a loving, supportive family or with advantages that can bring opportunities that others may not have, giving back is vital. Volunteering is something that has been an integral part of my life since I was young. My mother set a wonderful example of volunteering for our church as well as non-profit organizations in our community. She was kindhearted and always willing to do for others, especially the less fortunate. I am grateful for her and that she led me to do the same in my life. Humanitarian efforts are a strong focus for me personally. If I can help another person to make their life better, I get a great sense of fulfillment. I feel very blessed to be where I am in my life, and being able to help others less fortunate is important for me.

As I shared in the opening of this chapter, living well will look different to everyone. For me, it has been about my life journey—mind, body, and soul. Our personal experiences shape us and make up who we are as unique individuals.

I am grateful for the opportunity to contribute to a book about living well and what it means to me. I hope that my story resonates with someone and helps those who have struggled with health issues in their life to know that they are not alone. We are all going through something, and it helps to remember that when we encounter others.

With close to 20 years of experience in employee benefits, including the provider, carrier, and human resources (HR) space, Julie brings a multi-pronged approach to help employers navigate the complex health insurance environment. Julie brings a strong pharmacy benefit background and experience working with jumbo employers. She can help employers tackle their highest healthcare costs through learned strategies from some of the largest companies in the nation.

Julie's extensive body of work and insatiable appetite for learning make her a strong, dedicated business partner. She is constantly looking for opportunities to connect those in her network and find ways to help her clients grow.

Julie's time in the HR consulting space allowed for continuous professional development, including the Brené Brown Dare to Lead™ program, which has been the most impactful training in her career.

In 2016, Julie joined the National Human Resources Association and was quickly asked to join their board of directors. She spent two years in the president role and continues to sit on the board today.

Please scan the QR code to connect with this author.

Deanna Finch

I Said Yes

My leadership journey is a winding one. One that could not be predicted by birth order or social-economic status. Not one backed by academia, but one that is backed by personal lived experience. I am a leader who has known failure, setbacks, and crises along with success, wins, and triumphs—both professionally and personally. I am a leader who said yes when given a chance, and I am extremely proud of my journey because of the lessons I have learned and can share.

Experiencing the loss of a parent at a young age and the nearly equally traumatic events in the aftermath made navigating life more difficult for me. I was born and raised in poverty in the foothills of Missouri. Add early childhood trauma and grief with the death of my parent; displacement from my childhood home, friends and family; a replacement family in a new town four months after my dad's death; sexual grooming, assault, and rape as an adolescent; observance of domestic abuse; and poor maternal mental health with attempts at suicide to the mix, and you get a predictable outcome: depression, anxiety, high school dropout, running away from home to get married at 17, and early pregnancy. Later, multiple divorces, starting/stopping college, bankruptcy, homelessness, depression, drug and alcohol abuse, and despair. The first 30 years of my life followed textbook research and statistics on the effects of negative childhood experiences. However, despite facing adversity, I often discover opportunities on the other side of challenges.

Enrolling in cosmetology school after getting my GED was one way I knew I could survive with a skill that I could take with me no matter what else happened to me. It was hairdressing that taught me how to run a business, how to truly listen to people, and how to negotiate with them to get the best results that met their needs. I didn't just color and cut their hair. I listened to them, affirmed and loved them, bringing out their confidence and beauty inside of them. It is why my business tagline was "inner beauty, outer glow." I loved being a hairdresser because of the women I got to feed into and make a difference in their lives. There were three salon owners that mentored me who helped shape me as a leader. All of them had big hearts for people—their clients and their employees. They each took me under their wings, and I watched them, taking in everything I could learn from them. Not just the skill and art of hairdressing, but the secret to a good business—continuous learning, growth, and, most importantly, making a positive impact in the clients' lives.

When I got divorced the first time, at 21, my son was 2, and hairdressing alone wasn't going to provide what my son and I needed. I needed to go back to school with a quick turnaround to get started. I chose a school that offered an associate's degree in paralegal studies in less than two years. When I graduated, I worked for a lawyer in Clayton, Missouri, and she was a badass. It was just her, another paralegal, and me. At the time, I had never seen a strong, bold, fearless woman who wouldn't back down from a fight for justice until I worked for her. As a paralegal, I got to fight for victims of sexual harassment and sex, racial, and religious discrimination. I helped grieving families navigate the probate system. I learned about mediation and negotiation. In the 4 years I was a paralegal,

I learned so much about the world, about business, and just enough about law to get me into trouble. What drove me every day was learning something new and helping clients get justice.

I was married again by the time I was 24. We were madly in love. It was different than my first marriage, where I was running away from a traumatic house and to a stable, loving family. We bought a house, had plenty of food on the table, and were happy. We started talking about having kids. I knew that if I were to have more kids, I would want to stay home with them for the first few years. My son was just starting kindergarten, and I wanted to be able to be there after school, be a room mother, and chaperone the field trips. I made the decision to quit my job as a paralegal and go back to doing hair on the side as more of a hobby for extra cash. I opened my own salon and spa in 2007. We were married for 5 years by then. Things were good. And then they weren't. The market crashed, and my clients cut back on luxuries. The original business plan I created flew out the door with everyone's credit scores. My husband lost his job. I was back in survival trauma mode, and my body was familiar with it. I worked harder and longer. I was working 12 hours a day, 6-7 days a week, just to keep the business's doors open. By 2010, my husband left. This wasn't what he signed up for. He left me in the late summer with the house and a car that I could not afford with a failing business. That next December, I remember asking someone to come over to my house to put up plastic sheeting and covers over the windows and to make a barricade of sheets and covers around the living room where we had a fireplace so that I could keep the heat in since the electric was shut off. I had to abandon my house, and I lost my car.

I tried living with my brother, sister-in-law, and their two teenagers. I tried living with my mom again. I floated around until my friend/client offered me a deal. I could use one of their cars in exchange for free haircuts and services for her family, and I could pay $100 to live in a trailer on their property. The trailer wasn't much, but at least it was a place of my own. I never cooked in the kitchen because mice were the permanent residents in the cabinets. The squirrels played rugby on the metal roof at night, and I never got a full night's sleep. I was getting exhausted with life itself. No one would have thought I was as low as I was. I learned from a very early age how to mask my depression. I learned how to make people laugh, how to dress like I was happy and successful, and how to put on a good show to make sure everyone felt comfortable.

The only thing I knew to do was work harder and more. I was not willing to give up until someone finally told me the truth—the unabashed, ugly truth. The business was not failing because of my effort. It was just failing. That's it. It wasn't deeper than that. It had nothing to do with my intelligence, my skill, my education, my personality, my past, what anyone said or thought about me, or anything else that was swarming around in my trauma brain. I could not help that the market crashed in 2008, and people had not recovered from it yet in 2011. There was nothing else I could do, and the sooner I could admit it, the sooner I could move on to a decision that would impact the rest of my life leading me to write a chapter in a book about it today. This someone opened my eyes to see that I deserved to think about what served my needs first, and as soon as I did, the universe provided an opening.

I said yes, and I didn't look back. I closed the salon and said yes to an opportunity to work at an engineering firm in St. Louis, of all industries to enter. I used my business acumen and paralegal skills to take an office manager role. I leaned into my love of learning and need to know how things work and learned as much as I could about heavy industrial engineering. I said yes when given the opportunity to write inspection reports. I said yes when the owner offered me the first business development position for the St. Louis regional office to help them expand. I was the only female in most rooms, and that was not a position of privilege in that industry. I had to prove myself more than the men, but I was up to the challenge.

As I networked, I met people who introduced me to United 4 Children. I was ready to give back to something other than myself, so when I was asked to join the board of directors, I said yes. A year later, the fundraising position opened at United 4 Children. I had already fallen in love with the mission. I was able to connect the cause to my own childhood and my life as a parent navigating poverty and trauma with a child with challenging behaviors. They talked about adverse childhood experiences and how childcare providers who they trained and coached served as buffers to children's trauma by learning how to nurture and teach them social-emotional skills that would build their resilience. I knew that if I had known about United 4 Children before my son went to kindergarten, I would have been more confident in asking questions and asking for resources necessary to support him. I thought that every parent should know about United 4 Children and wanted to help make that happen. I raised my hand and said yes! They said yes, too.

I had a slim chance of becoming a high-achieving executive in St. Louis when I started my journey, but I'm happy to announce that when someone gives you a chance, and you take it, trajectories can change. It's been 10 years since I became a board member at United 4 Children. I've been the Executive Director for 6 years, and I have been living my best life yet. I have finally stopped asking why I had to go through all of the hardship and suffering in my first 30 years. Learning about the work of United 4 Children helped me make sense of my own life, and it came into my life just in time. Some of the stories or lessons I share with my team today to tackle a business, team, or client problem are some of the stories and lessons I acquired as a hairdresser. I still have that same justice-seeking need I had when I was a paralegal, but with a little more resolution and self-confidence, and like the lawyer I learned from, I don't back down from a fight.

For a long time, I wanted to bury my past, ashamed of what people would think of me. But now, I know that the grit within me is what is required for the next 30 years of adventure, and I plan on leading it with all the stories of growth, resiliency, intention, and tenacity I have acquired. I will keep acquiring stories, sharing them, saying yes, and living my best life so that I can possibly help someone else best live theirs.

Deanna Finch is the executive director of United 4 Children, which serves more than 34,000 children, families, and childcare providers each year in Missouri. She leads the nonprofit›s team as they advance their vision to ensure that every child has the foundation to thrive. Before becoming executive director, Deanna worked as the organization's development officer and event director and previously served on the United 4 Children's board of directors. Deanna has more than a decade of experience in business development and nonprofit leadership. Deanna is an alumna of FOCUS St. Louis cohorts, Women in Leadership #75 and Leadership St. Louis #48. She is passionate about improving the health and well-being of children and families across Missouri.

Please scan the QR code to connect with this author.

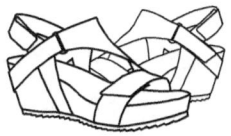

Kristen Ziegler

The Transformative Power of Curiosity and Courage

Growing up in a small farm town, I got to spend my childhood playing in the lakes and creeks, making forts in the woods, racing row boats with my cousins across the family lake, and having Sunday fish fries at Grandma's house, where our family would gather to enjoy the latest catch of the week.

The middle of three children, I was the daughter of two school-teachers. My dad also coached high school football and wrestling. I spent a lot of time around other educators, and they never seemed to mind that I was a very curious child. I was extremely empathetic before I knew there was a word for it, and often studied non-verbal cues.

My interest in understanding others continued as I grew older. After high school, I pursued a bachelor's degree with the determination to stand out from my peers as I prepared to start a career. My strategy was to create my own internship opportunities so I could get the experience I wanted, rather than applying to active job postings that didn't excite me. Creating opportunities and believing in myself was just part of the equation. Having support from influential people who believed in me was the other.

My tenacious nature led to jobs with the federal government and another that allowed me to evaluate and counsel criminals in a maximum-security facility under the direction of a forensic psychiatrist. I ultimately decided to become a police officer and criminal investigator to help people experiencing traumatic events. No one in my family had ever been in that type of career before, and there were not many women in the field, especially in rural areas of the Midwest in the '90s. Nonetheless, I was drawn to it and my father had me convinced I could do anything I wanted to do in life. To this day, I am still not sure why I chose law enforcement. Maybe it chose me.

As a rookie officer, only 21 years old, and the only woman on the force at that time, it quickly became apparent that I needed to prove myself worthy of my position if I was going to be respected or valued as a fellow officer. I was hired by a police chief who believed I would succeed, but I heard horror stories of other women who had been hired as officers only to be run off because the other officers didn't think women could handle themselves on the street. I was determined to be successful, and although it felt like a scary uphill battle, I sure as heck wasn't about to let anyone run me off. I had to learn how to adapt to conditions within seconds, from one emergency to the next, while experiencing the emotional fluctuations that occur when facing danger, de-escalating fights, trying to save lives, and protecting my own. I would always rush to be the first one to the scene and make sure I was the last one to leave unless a priority call came. I offered to cover shifts, come in early or stay late, and learned as much as I could from other officers.

I remember one of my first experiences with death when I received a call about a six-year-old girl. When I arrived, I felt a sense of peace knowing that she was no longer in pain, but the sadness and pain I felt for her family, who were still trying to save her, seemed almost unbearable. If it felt that terrible to me, I could only imagine the agony they must be experiencing. I looked over at my training officer and was confused when I could not interpret how he was feeling. I vividly recall that, at that particular moment, I told myself that I needed to learn how to do the same. I coped by imagining the death scene as a movie, not real life, so I could stay strong for the family while shielding my emotions and vulnerabilities.

Intellectually, I knew that death was a natural part of life and not everyone could be saved. However, emotionally, I could not have prepared myself for the sense of helplessness I felt. Whatever I did to armor myself that day stayed with me for a long time until I was able to better manage the constant flux of emotional turmoil on the job.

I'll never forget the day I stopped trying to prove myself.

I had just returned to the police station after working a vehicle accident, and my brain was still trying to process the circumstances. The victim was an elderly woman, severely injured and trapped in her car. Her daughter and grandkids had been following in the car behind and witnessed the accident. As I waited for fire and EMS to arrive, I stayed close to her, and it seemed like an eternity as we maintained eye contact. No words were spoken for several seconds, but there was a calm about her gaze. I felt like she was telling me she was okay, no matter what happened, without using words. It was a strange sensation. Suddenly, I heard the crying screams of her granddaughter who was about as tall as my knees and pulling on the right pant leg of my uniform. She was begging me to help her grandma, and she wasn't old enough to understand that I could not get her grandma out of the vehicle without special equipment and assistance. It didn't matter though. She wanted me to fix it, to save her grandma. To this day, I still wonder if she thinks of me as the officer who could not save her grandma.

As I was about to sit down to write my accident report, another officer was coming on duty. He was a well-respected officer and the kind that everyone wanted as backup when responding to calls. He stopped and looked at me for a few seconds and said, "You know, every time I see you, I have to wonder whether or not you would be able to pull me from a dangerous scene if I was injured or if you would just get scared and run away." I walked closer to him, looked him directly in the eyes, and said, "You know what, officer? Every time I see you, I wonder the same things about you."

That day, I met my self-worth and never again felt like I had to prove myself to the other officers. I knew my capabilities, I understood my mission in the communities I served, and that was enough.

My ten-year career in law enforcement was invaluable to my personal and professional growth. The daily micro-interactions with people from all walks of life and the intricate dynamics of criminal investigations provided me with a deep understanding of human nature, rarely gleaned from most professions. My mission was to be a voice for the victims, even those who no longer had a voice, and navigating human behavior is where I excelled. I later became a lead criminal investigator, trained other officers, and received state recognition for my ability to solve and obtain confessions during homicide and arson investigations, leading to successful convictions.

I miss the camaraderie of law enforcement and the daily conversations that only someone in law enforcement would truly understand, but I am still close with my former chief and brothers in blue. I cannot think of any other career that would have better prepared me to grow into the version of me that was needed for the rest of my journey.

I married my first husband at my father's bedside, just a few days before my father passed away from cancer. In my twenties, the thought of losing a parent was the worst possible thing I could imagine. Still in law enforcement at the time, my fellow officers contacted the county Sheriff's department that held jurisdiction where my parents lived. They asked and received permission from the Sheriff's Department to be the agency leading the funeral procession from the funeral home to our family cemetery. Each squad car parked at key intersections along the route to stop traffic, and my brothers in blue stood at parade rest next to their cars, as we passed. My dad was my hero, and this was a pivotal moment in my life because it changed my perception of the world and relationships. I believed the bar on my resiliency barometer had been set pretty high already, and after this, I was confident I would be able to conquer any challenge or endure any pain that came my way. The day I lost my dad, I drew on his belief in me and used it to embrace life and fuel my journey from that day forward.

The greatest moment of my life happened when I gave birth to my beautiful daughter, less than two years after my dad left this physical world. The following years brought about numerous changes and new beginnings.

Experiencing a life with Dad no longer in it. Worrying about my siblings and how they were coping, and my mom as she was learning to live alone. Finishing my master's degree. Starting a new job as I transitioned from law enforcement to the corporate world of security and executive protection for a global brewing company. Moving into a different home after going through a divorce, feeling like a failure for getting divorced, and navigating life as a single mother. Through each change, whether it felt good or bad, I just knew that I had to figure this out and make it work. I had no ultimate plan but knew that the most important thing was being a mother first. I wanted my daughter to see that everyone, even single moms, could empower themselves within. So, I pushed through all the self-defeating emotions and fears I was feeling inside and persisted.

When I started my new job, the corporate world looked like a playground of opportunities to keep helping people. The way I helped would be different but still important and impactful. Coming from a police background, I had respect for titles and the chain of command and was accustomed to being part of a very strong team of humans who worked together to solve the most complex problems imaginable. I had already faced life and death many times, and I knew that nothing I could face in a corporate job would come close to being that difficult.

When I stepped into the corporate environment, one of the first things that caught my attention was how job titles influenced people's perceptions of each other and, sometimes, themselves. It was evident that job titles could stifle career growth if people failed to acknowledge the full range of talents others possessed. To me, a title helped identify subject matter experts, but it simply represented the role someone was fulfilling for the company at any given time. I made a mental note to never let my title limit my worth to an organization and to never let someone else's title limit my perception of their capabilities.

I intentionally forged a unique and somewhat uncharted career path for myself. If the thought of something new made me feel slightly uncomfortable, I learned to embrace the discomfort to continue learning. I searched for the next unknown to explore and discovered new strengths as I summoned every ounce of courage I could find to continually push my own boundaries.

For the next eleven years, I wore many hats and learned something from everyone I met. I later learned that I was the first person in the company's history to transfer from a security and executive protection-focused role to a corporate human resources (HR) position, which was completely outside of the security realm. The head of the People Team had confidence in me, and he gave me my first opportunity in the HR world.

Applying my understanding of human behavior to drive corporate strategies quickly became a passion. It became clear that leveraging this knowledge to communicate effectively, drive the right behaviors, influence decisions, and achieve successful outcomes was crucial. I recognized the intersection of my passion and career and could connect the dots along my journey that prepared me for today.

I didn't do anything particularly special to advance my career. I simply made connections, developed relationships, and repeatedly asked the same question: "What else can I do to help here?" Each time I asked, I was presented with new opportunities and people who believed I could do it.

Today, I am the Chief Human Resources Officer for an incredible organization and a small business owner in the transportation industry. I am married to the love of my life, have two bonus sons, and my daughter is completing her senior year at university.

When I reflect on the people, the events, and the choices that influenced each step of my journey, I recognize how empowered we are to harness the energy of every experience and choose what to do with it.

I choose to live with curiosity and courage, embracing the transformative power unique to human connections.

From an early age, Kristen Ziegler demonstrated a deep sense of empathy, always drawn to helping others. This initially led her to a career in law enforcement, where she built a foundation of courage, adaptability, leadership, and conflict-resolution skills. Along the way, she faced significant challenges, often navigating male-dominated spaces and overcoming barriers to success. Undeterred, she embraced every obstacle as an opportunity to grow. In her twenties, she faced a profound loss with the passing of her father. His unwavering belief in her became a powerful force that fueled her journey from that day forward. Her curiosity and desire to make a broader impact inspired a transition into human resources.

Today, Kristen is a highly respected HR professional known for her exceptional emotional intelligence and her ability to create inclusive workplaces where people feel heard and valued. Her background uniquely qualifies her to solve complex organizational challenges with empathy, authenticity, and determination.

Please scan the QR code to connect with this author.

Arrah Karigan

Intuition: Grit's Quiet Guide

"It's none of my business what you think of me."

When I first heard this, I was in my mid-twenties, and the statement seemed absurd. How could it *not* be my business? My entire life up to that point felt like an intricate balancing act, ensuring I managed how others perceived me. How I was seen—competent, successful, agreeable—seemed crucial to my existence. It was my way of staying safe, of being liked, of avoiding conflict. Letting go of that control felt impossible, even reckless.

But as time passed, I began to realize how revolutionary that statement really was. More importantly, I came to understand how much freedom it held. It challenged everything I thought I knew about myself and the world around me. The practice of unpacking the idea that I was not responsible for managing other people's thoughts was like loosening the tight grip I'd held over my own identity for so long. It opened a door into a new way of being, one that would lead to a journey of growth, resilience, intention, and most importantly, tenacity—the kind of tenacity it takes to truly live your own life, to follow your intuition, no matter how inconvenient or at odds it may be with others' expectations.

For years, I had been living with an underlying fear of rejection—of not being enough, not fitting in, or not living up to my family's ideals.

Growing up in a Southern family, there were unwritten but powerful rules about what it meant to be a "good" person, a "good" daughter, a "good" woman. I carried these expectations with me, and the idea of stepping outside those lines was terrifying. To make decisions based solely on my inner guidance, to follow my intuition even when it ran counter to what my family thought I should do, felt like stepping off a cliff without knowing where I would land.

Then I met my husband, and life shifted dramatically. We met on vacation, an encounter that would soon transform into a deep partnership. At first, the excitement of a new relationship, combined with the novelty of marriage, was exhilarating. But the honeymoon phase ended quickly, and we found ourselves thrust into what I can only describe as "the work" of life. This was where true growth began—and with it, the tests of resilience and tenacity. I had left my home state, my entire support system, and had become a stepmom almost overnight.

Life moved quickly, and before long, I was navigating everything from financial audits to miscarriages. It was one trial after another, and all the while, I was still struggling with that ingrained habit of trying to control how others perceived me. Even in these challenging moments, I found myself slipping into old patterns, trying to appear strong and capable when I was anything but. I was trying to assimilate into a new life in the Midwest, a place where hospitality and communication felt unfamiliar, and my Southern roots often seemed at odds with the social nuances I encountered.

Yet, despite all the external chaos, something inside me was beginning to shift. My intuition—the quiet, persistent voice that had always been there—began to grow louder. But listening to that voice required space. It required silence. It required the discipline of stillness, which I had been cultivating for years before this next level of my life. Meditation is the anchor that grounded me through all of life's turbulence. It wasn't just a daily habit; it became my sanctuary, my chance to stop the relentless noise of trying to control everything, including other people's opinions. It was an opportunity to thank God for loving me even when I felt unworthy and ashamed.

In the midst of the chaos, I carved out small moments of silence. These moments were non-negotiable. Even when everything else felt impossible, when life felt like it was closing in on me, I made time to sit, to breathe, and to listen. It was in these quiet spaces that I learned the most valuable lesson: resilience is not about pushing through or soldiering on; it's about surrender. It's about making room for intuition, for that quiet, inner knowing that has always been there. In meditation, I began to hear my own voice again, unclouded by the noise of others' expectations.

Then, in September 2019, I gave birth to my daughter. While I had longed for her, nothing could have prepared me for the tidal wave that followed. The postpartum depression and anxiety that set in was like nothing I had ever experienced. It was as though my mind had been taken over by something dark and overwhelming. The practice of meditation, which had been a source of comfort before, now became essential. It was through meditation that I learned to make space for my mental health—to acknowledge that mental health is *real* health, that it's not a choice when something goes awry. I couldn't control what was happening, but I could create space to navigate it.

During those early months of motherhood, my baby was colicky and miserable for what felt like an eternity—five months of endless crying. My husband was at work, and I was alone with this tiny being, struggling through the days. I deeply regretted my decision to quit my job and stay home. It would have been easier, I thought, to go to work than to face the relentless demands of a newborn. I was adrift, and all I wanted was some semblance of peace.

Once again, I found myself at a crossroads. I could give in to the despair, to the self-pity that was always lurking at the edges, or I could reach out. I chose the latter. I joined a mom's group at my church, and while it seemed like a small act at the time, it was a pivotal one. This was a decision born out of intention—the intention to heal, to grow, to connect. In the group, I found friendship, community, and, most importantly, a space where I could be vulnerable. Through these women, my Rad Moms, I learned that I didn't have to carry the weight of everything alone. I learned that it's okay to need help, to need others, to ask for support.

When the pandemic hit, those relationships became a lifeline. We would bundle up in sleeping bags and sit on patios in the bitter St. Louis cold just to maintain some form of human connection. It was through these moments that I understood the true meaning of resilience. Resilience isn't about enduring hardship silently; it's about showing up, even when things are hard. It's about having the tenacity to keep moving forward, to make intentional choices even when life feels overwhelming.

In those moments of stillness, through the practice of meditation, I continued to hear my intuition guiding me. I learned that intuition isn't always convenient. It doesn't always lead me down the easiest path. But it does lead me to the right path, to the path that's meant for *me*. I began to understand that my worth wasn't tied to how others saw me or even to how I perceived myself during moments of struggle. My worth was inherent, simply in being, in showing up to life as authentically as I could.

In 2021, my life took yet another unexpected turn when I was abruptly terminated from my employer. It felt as though my world had been turned upside down. Again. I had already weathered so many storms, but each time, the upheaval still caught me off guard. Yet, as always, my intuition was close by, quietly guiding me. I knew what I had to do, even though the path ahead wasn't going to be easy. Listening to that inner voice is often nerve-wracking, especially when it asks us to take risks or go against the grain of what feels safe or familiar. But I had the temerity to stay the course.

Looking back, I can see clearly that this big, scary event was God doing for me what I had been unable to do for myself. Had it been up to me, I don't know that I would've had the courage to leave on my own. I certainly wouldn't have been able to get away as cleanly or completely. But in that abrupt ending, there was a strange grace. The time and space that followed allowed me to rest, to recuperate, and to simply be a mom to my now delightful child. It was a much-needed pause, a time to reflect and integrate everything I had been through.

It was through meditation and mindfulness that I learned the art of letting go—letting go of the need to manage others' perceptions, to control the uncontrollable. I learned that there is deep wisdom in surrender, in allowing life to unfold rather than forcing it into a specific shape. And in that letting go, I made room for something more powerful: growth. I began to grow into the person I had always been but hadn't allowed myself to fully become.

During that period of reflection, something unexpected happened: an idea started to take shape. I had long been passionate about the healing power of meditation and mindfulness, and it became clear to me that this was a gift I was meant to share with others. With the extra time I had, I founded my own consulting company—Higher State Consulting—dedicated to spreading the practice of meditation to those who needed it most. It felt like a natural extension of the work I had been doing within myself, and now, I had the opportunity to offer that same gift to others.

This was yet another reminder of the importance of following my intuition, no matter how inconvenient or difficult the path may seem. In the face of loss and uncertainty, I was given the chance to rebuild my life with intention. It was a testament to the power of resilience and the tenacity required to navigate life's twists and turns. And through it all, my practice of meditation remained my savior, my constant anchor, guiding me to what was next—even when I couldn't see the way forward.

And then, perhaps the most humbling lesson of all, I learned that I *cannot* do it all, and more importantly, that I don't have to. In trying to manage everything, I had been denying others the opportunity to step in, to show up for me, and to love me. Dropping some of the balls, as terrifying as it felt at first, allowed my husband, my friends, and my community to show me love in ways I hadn't even known I needed.

Growth, I've come to realize, doesn't happen in a vacuum. It happens in the space we create through mindfulness and intentional living. Resilience isn't about being unbreakable; it's about being willing to bend, to adapt, to let go when necessary, and to keep going with purpose. Intuition doesn't always shout; it often whispers. But in the stillness of meditation, I've learned to hear those whispers, to trust them, and to follow them.

The life I'm living now isn't perfect, but it's mine. It's messy, complicated, and filled with challenges, but it's also deeply authentic and intentional. I'm no longer consumed by what others think of me, and I'm not living my life according to anyone else's script. My practice of meditation has given me the clarity to see what matters most and the tenacity to follow my own path, no matter how hard or inconvenient it might seem.

In the end, the most important relationship we have is the one we cultivate with ourselves. Through a deep trust of my intuition, I've learned that I am enough, exactly as I am. And I've come to realize that what others think of me really *is* none of my business. My business is showing up for life with intention, resilience, and an unwavering trust in my own inner guidance. That's more than enough.

Arrah, a Louisiana native now living in St. Louis, founded Higher State Consulting in 2021 to help others cultivate mindfulness and meditation skills. Her work is driven by a deep belief in the power of presence to transform lives, offering guidance to those seeking greater clarity and calm. In her personal life, Arrah enjoys gardening, yoga, reading, baking, and riding horses, all of which help her stay grounded and connected. She treasures long walks with friends and time with her family—her husband Brad, children Jameson and Christian, and niece Mattie. Mindfulness for Arrah is not just a practice, but a way of living with intention and joy.

Please scan the QR code to connect with this author.

Nicole Powell

A Suitcase and a Basket of Chocolate

From T-Shirts to Winter Coats

It was December 26, 1991, the day after Christmas, when most families were likely still knee-deep in wrapping paper and distracted by their newest gadgets. For me, it was a bittersweet day as I said goodbye to the family and life I knew in Manila, Philippines, and arrived in America with my father and suitcase in hand to be reunited with my mom to begin our new life in "the States."

Despite having vivid memories of a journey made 33 years ago, I can't recall what I actually brought with me from Manila—just the giant black suitcase, which I now realize symbolizes everything I was leaving behind and everything I hoped to gain in this new land. My first memory is stepping out into the biting cold of winter, something I had never experienced before. I was unprepared for the freezing air that greeted me in New York City. It was then that I learned what a winter coat was as my mother handed me a black coat with different colored pockets, an item that would become essential in this new chapter of life.

But what stands out most vividly from that first night wasn't the cold or the bright lights of the cars as we entered the Bronx—it was a basket of chocolates sitting in the apartment where we were staying. A simple wicker basket, overflowing with more chocolates than I had ever seen in my life. That basket epitomized my early idea of America: a land of abundance and Mickey Mouse, toys and treats for the taking. I didn't know it then, but that basket of chocolates would become a metaphor for my entire journey—a journey of striving, struggling, and ultimately, succeeding in creating my own version of the American dream.

December 26, 1991

Ask me what I did last week, and I have to admit I'd be stumped. I can, however, vividly recall the events of December 26, 1991. I was filled with a mix of excitement and sadness. We were leaving behind a life we knew —one with its own challenges but also comforts: like a home filled with family, including one of my favorite people, my grandpa. In exchange, we were reunited with my wonderful mother, Emmeline. She left Manila for New York in hopes of starting a new life as a nurse, with the goal of eventually bringing us to America. It was a goal she achieved, and I thank her every day for it.

At six years old, I didn't care too much for symbolism. Fast forward to now and I realize the suitcase I carried that day represented uncertainty. As we made our way to a small apartment, I hoped that everything left behind could somehow be regained in this new place.

Imagine my surprise and excitement when I walked through the door and my eyes immediately fell on a basket of chocolates sitting at the end of the hallway. It was overflowing with every kind of chocolate you could think of wrapped in colorful foil. Brands I had never heard of! It was the most chocolate I had ever seen. To me, it was a symbol of America's abundance, a visual representation of the images and TV shows I watched in our living room in the Philippines.

That basket became a touchstone for my early experience in America. I remember thinking, "This is what America is like—everything you could ever want, all in one place." In my young mind, America was a place where dreams came true, where even the smallest things, like chocolates, were available in endless supply.

The Mouse is to Blame

As a child, my image of America was largely shaped by television and movies. Mickey Mouse, Disneyland, and the people I saw on TV—who looked so different from me—were my first introductions to the idea of "Americans" and the "American dream." I imagined a place where anything was possible, where hard work was always rewarded, and where people lived in harmony with an abundance of everything: money, food, and success. America was like Willy Wonka's Factory, and I was Charlie—humbled by the invitation and excited to embrace it all.

The vision of the American dream that formed in my mind was one of fame, wealth, brand names, expansive front yards, and having titles before your name like VP or EVP. The goal was to be popular, marry Zack Morris, and get good grades so you could attend the fanciest of colleges. These images stuck with me, shaping my expectations of what success looked like in the U.S.

The basket of chocolates was the validation of those fantasies for both six-year-old and, eventually, young adult Nicole. Once the naivety of childhood melted away, I realized the basket of chocolates still held significance in my life, serving as a metaphor for my American experience. At first, I was awed by the abundance in front of me, but I didn't realize that some candies might not be to my liking—some would be bitter or not what I expected. Similarly, America, despite its great opportunities, had underlying issues of its own. Yet, I had to keep unwrapping each piece, pushing through the disappointments, until I found the ones that were made for me and my taste buds, much like the experiences and opportunities I discovered along the way.

The Pressure to be Perfectly American

"Guanloao? Guanloa? Guanlo… Sorry, how do you pronounce your name?"

I heard this often, even right before I walked on stage during my college graduation. My maiden name is Guanlao (pronounced Gwan-LAH-o), and people continuously struggled to pronounce it correctly. It seemed like a small thing, but it was a constant reminder that I was different. I would cringe every time someone stumbled over it, feeling a mix of embarrassment and frustration. It drove me crazy that something as simple as a name could make me feel so out of place, even in a borough as diverse as the Bronx.

Was the real American dream only for those born in America? Since I wasn't born here, did I have to do everything possible to appear fully American, even though I didn't look like the people I saw on television? How could I climb the corporate ladder if I didn't know anyone who had taken those steps and could guide me on the best path to follow? These were the questions I asked myself as I crumbled under the pressure to assimilate. I wanted so badly to fit in. I wanted to speak like an American, dress like an American, and most of all, be accepted as one of them. But no matter how hard I tried, there were always reminders that I wasn't from here.

I fought hard against the idea that I didn't belong. I wanted so badly to prove that I could live the American dream, that I could be just as successful as anyone born here. Yet no matter how much I tried to fit in, there was always a part of me that felt like an outsider.

Breaking Through the "American Dream"

The image of that basket of chocolates—a land of abundance where anything seemed possible—stayed with me, pushing me to keep striving, to keep moving forward. There were moments when the dream felt out of reach, but I pressed on, driven by the belief that it could still be mine.

Back then, my idea of the American dream was tied to what I saw on TV as a child—fame, wealth, fancy clothes, and a prestigious title. I thought that if I could achieve those things, I'd have truly "made it" in this country. But as I chased those goals, something felt off. It seemed like the exit sign leading to the "American Dream" kept moving further and further away. Then, something inside me began to shift.

As I reflected on my journey, I realized that the dream I had been chasing—fame, wealth, and brand names—wasn't what truly mattered. I let go of the need for those external markers of success and began focusing on what truly brought me joy and fulfillment.

I realized my "American Dream" was about having the freedom to choose—choosing my path, navigating life with intention, and having the ability to change course when needed. I embraced the freedom to switch gears, change directions, and take action.

I let go of the traditional idea of the "American Dream" and replaced it with "My Dream"—Nicole's Dream. I prioritized my happiness and gratitude. I stopped always looking ahead and instead started appreciating the present. I may not have a corporate-given fancy title or make millions of dollars, but 33 years later, I'm here—healthy, happy, and grateful for the choices I've made.

I built a business from the ground up, created a career, and made connections in an industry where I had once felt like a complete outsider. The values I learned from my immigrant upbringing—hard work, resilience, and perseverance—became the foundation for building my business. When I shifted my perspective, I realized that I had already achieved so much more than I had ever dreamed of as a child. I took advantage of the opportunities that came my way and created something meaningful—something I'm proud of.

A New Basket

Now that I'm a parent, I think a lot about the legacy I want to leave for my children. I want them to understand where they come from and to remember the culture and country that shaped me. I don't want them to feel the pressure to assimilate as I did. Instead, I want them to embrace their heritage while creating their own version of the dream.

I've worked hard to build a life that honors both my past and my present, and I want my children to do the same. I want them to understand that success isn't about fitting in or achieving material wealth—it's about staying true to who they are.

I want their basket to be filled with seeds, not colorfully wrapped chocolates—seeds that, when nurtured, grow into a variety of sweet and flavorful fruits, like apples, oranges, and mangoes. These seeds must be tended with care and patience, showing them that true rewards come from effort and dedication. Nothing in life is instantaneous; the fruits of their labor will only come with time, hard work, and perseverance.

Redefining Living Well

As I look back on my journey, I realize that living well is a choice. Every day, I made the decision to keep going, to keep striving, to keep believing in the dream I had as a child. Living well wasn't just about achieving success—it was about making choices that aligned with my values, taking action to create the life I wanted, and refusing to resign myself to the idea that I didn't belong.

I chose to believe in my ability to create a life for myself and my family, even when I felt discouraged. And in doing so, I created my own version of the American dream—one that honors my roots and allows me to live well on my own terms. And that, I believe, is the true essence of not just the American dream, but our collective dream.

Nicole Powell, a certified brand strategist and expert in neuromarketing, is the founder of HALCON Marketing Solutions, a marketing agency that designs cutting-edge branding and marketing strategies for businesses across diverse sectors. With over 16 years of experience, Nicole has worked with small and mid-sized businesses as well as major media giants like Viacom, ESPN, and Fox Networks, spearheading transformative campaigns for high-profile clients. Her insights have been showcased in publications such as *USA Today, Yahoo! Finance, Business Insider,* and local news outlets. Passionate about building and empowering teams, Nicole's approach emphasizes creativity, collaboration, and cooperation. Her mission is to revolutionize the marketing industry by fostering a culture where creativity and community go hand in hand, while driving exceptional business growth.

Please scan the QR code to connect with this author.

Cheryl A. Houston, PhD

Teacher, I Feel the Dots Connecting

In April 2018, my husband was involved in a very serious car accident that changed the course of our lives, just two weeks after we met with a real estate broker, real estate agent, and a loan officer in San Diego to put our retirement plans in motion. Plans that were eleven years in the making. As the trauma team assessed the extent of the damages to my husband's battered and broken body, I felt the sheer terror at the thought of losing him and the intense grief of knowing that our retirement plans were slipping through my fingers like the sand on my favorite Southern California beach. Many broken bones, including two fractured cervical discs and a traumatic brain injury…it could have been much worse. I rarely left his side as he spent ten days in the ICU, two weeks in the TCU, and just over three weeks each in inpatient rehab, followed by a skilled nursing facility. On Day 70, just four days prior to his release to home, I received shocking news of my own that would *also* change the course of our lives. My gynecologist suspected that I had cancer. This started the journey of my lifetime into the unknown, where I learned slowly and steadily how to live well with G.R.I.T.—growth, resilience, intention, and tenacity.

In July 2018, I received a call from my oncologist as I was being dropped off at the hospital entrance to visit another specialist. "I'm so sorry to have to tell you this, Cheryl, after all you have been through these many months, but the pathology report confirmed that you have cancer." I wasn't at all surprised. I had been expecting these words my whole life. My maternal side of the family was no stranger to cancer. My mother and four of her five sisters, plus one of my three uncles, all developed cancer in their lifetime. Cancer treatment was brutal back in the '60s. My first memory of the havoc chemo and radiation wreak on the body occurred when I was only about 7 or 8 years old. I remember watching one dear relative after another repeat the same life-taxing process, submit to the installation of a port, succumb to the nausea and vomiting associated with chemo, lose their beautiful hair, and eventually relinquish their precious lives. I had maternal cousins who watched their mothers battle unsuccessfully with cancer, then developed cancer of their own in their 30s. I observed the cold, impersonal way that cancer took the life of one cousin who had to say goodbye to her four young children, sparing the children of the other cousin but leaving her wracked with survivor guilt. It's easy to understand why I felt receiving a cancer diagnosis was my genetic destiny. Only when I had the sophisticated testing in the 21st century did I come face to face with one reality: I didn't have a genetic predisposition for cancer. This was both a relief and a burden. A relief not to have to tell my two beautiful sons that they had a 50-50 chance of getting a cancer diagnosis in their lifetime. And a burden knowing that the way I chose to live my life put me at risk for this deadly disease. I had abused my body since college—a 23-year journey completing undergraduate, master's, and doctoral degrees, plus an internship. Burning the midnight oil studying set the stage after graduation into burning the midnight oil as an academic—grading papers, conducting research, and writing manuscripts in my accelerated pursuit of tenure. A habit of eating a bowl of M&Ms while studying as an undergraduate took root and transitioned into an addiction as I graded hundreds of my students' papers each academic year. The Freshman 15 snowballed into the Middle Aged 95—my weight tipping the scales above 200 pounds by the time I was 35. I ignored my body's pleas for relief, bathing myself in the hormones of stress, denying my need for adequate sleep, fueled by the obsession to succeed at all costs.

The doctor further revealed that I had a very rare cancer with a very poor prognosis. A cancer that doesn't flinch at chemo and doesn't acquiesce to radiation. And the chances of annual recurrence, he said was 50-70 percent. Left without a clear path to follow, I did the only thing I could do; I turned my education and training into an asset, scoured the literature for credible information, consulted with experts across the country, and looked tirelessly for the playbook that would guide me to good health. I believed that if my body made this cancer from decades of bad health habits, perhaps my body could heal this cancer with a lot of TLC.

It didn't take long for the playbook to appear. Dr. Kelly Turner, in her book titled, *Radical Remission*, shared the results of her direct interviews of over one hundred people and analyzed over a thousand written cases of individuals who stood toe to toe with cancer and received remission against all odds. Dr. Turner synthesized the information into nine healing factors that all of them applied to their lives, although not in the same fashion. In 2020, Dr. Turner updated the book, retitling it *Radical Hope*, and revealed that a 10th factor emerged from the data. She also updated the way she described each factor as follows.

1. Exercise
2. Spiritual Connection
3. Empowering Yourself
4. Increasing Positive Emotions
5. Following Your Intuition
6. Releasing Suppressed Emotions

7. Changing Your Diet

8. Herbs and Supplements

9. Having Strong Reasons for Living

10. Increasing Social Support

I didn't incorporate these healing factors in any specific order. I simply started with what was easiest and went from there. I also didn't do it alone. My first step in the right direction was to locate and team up with a brilliant integrative oncologist who also supported the healing factors described by Dr. Turner. He taught me the importance of creating a body terrain that was inhospitable to cancer development, and this meant following each factor with intentionality.

Relying on others and going all in with approaches that were largely unfamiliar to me was a hard lesson for me to learn. I often felt great pride in my self-sufficient mentality and training as an academic in health services research. But, I quickly realized that I needed to rely on others to get me through the ups and downs of the path I was taking and to trust. My cancer journey taught me first to ask for help, second to receive it with humility and grace, and third to be deeply grateful and look for ways to pay it forward. Just prior to my first surgery to remove the initial tumor, one of my former students helped me set up an account on the Lotsa Helping Hands website, and though I balked at first at this unfamiliar technology, it was a godsend! I invited everyone in my social circle to join and one of the best features was a sign-up calendar so that I didn't have to coordinate tasks and volunteers while I recovered. Another great feature was the wall; people uploaded inspirational quotes and encouragement, funny photos, and more.

Cancer helped me see very clearly what was important and what needed to be released. For example, when I first started thinking about my strong reasons for living. The first thing that popped into my head was my work and career. Ha! That was the old me; the new and wiser me now knows that my purpose is my family, and my two guiding values are time and energy, especially time spent with my two beautiful grandchildren, ages 4 and 8 at the time of this publication, and the energy to keep up with them as long as I can. These angels cracked open my heart, gave me numerous reasons to be grateful, and taught me how to unleash my inner child, long lost to the responsibilities of adulthood.

Some people in Dr. Turner's books expressed that cancer was a blessing. Others had described it as a gift. For me, cancer is my incessant teacher. It revealed to me that while the outside observer might have concluded that I seemed to have everything anyone could ask for, I was living a very unfulfilled life. Each time this teacher popped back up in my life was a reason to pause and connect the dots. I would reflect on how my thoughts were either supporting or degrading my body, the degree to which I was or wasn't following my healing path, adhering to my commitment to living my best and most authentic life, and whether I was making choices that put money in the bank vs. fed my soul.

This teacher challenged me to overcome some very deeply seated habits and ways of thinking and feeling. I learned to meditate consistently and be very comfortable sitting with my own monkey mind and observing whether my thoughts were true or a manifestation of fear, anxiety, and hypervigilance—the causes and conditions of my past. The quiet of these daily sits allowed me to cultivate and listen to my intuition. I no longer stayed up until the wee hours of the morning working. I understood the importance of rest and repair mode to support my physical body.

Perhaps the greatest growth occurred in my spiritual connection with Source. Thanks to programming through the Cancer Support Community of St. Louis, I was introduced to the practice of Zhineng Qigong. While I initially joined in for its ability to calm my anxiety about all the doom and gloom I was presented with by healthcare providers, it opened my heart to an inner knowing and truth about my authentic self. Other spiritual practices I employed included Healing Touch, sound baths, chanting, Metta, and earthing.

Thriving through a cancer diagnosis, whether you live with cancer or are blessed like I was for five years of reports that read, "No evidence of disease or metastasis," it's extremely important to cultivate resiliency and tenacity, especially as it relates to maintaining psychological well-being. For the first three years post-diagnosis, I had CT scans every three months. Learning to cope with "scanxiety" was initially very hard. Just as I started to relax and breathe, it seemed like it was time to be scanned again. My cancer psychologist reviewed my case history and suggested using the word "determined" to serve as my touchstone during these challenging times. Next, she encouraged me to live in the present moment and seek joy with others as a remedy. It started with humor. My husband playfully regarded my cancer as "the uninvited guest," and each surgery was deemed "Eviction Day." We watched our favorite comedians on Netflix and old reruns of shows that still made us laugh out loud. About a week prior to Scan Day, we reached out to everyone in my tribe by text, asking for positive vibes, prayers, and support. On the way to each scan, we sang songs from my Spotify playlist that I labeled "Badass Determined Thriver." And with each good report, we danced and cried in the doctor's office, broadcast our jubilation via text to our many supporters, and then stopped when we got home to breathe a sigh of grateful relief and hold each other tight before commencing with to-do lists of our lives.

Uterine leiomyosarcoma (uLMS) is impersonal and unrelenting, always looming in my life. The path forward has never been and never will be a straight line. With the help of my social support circle, I've learned to weather each setback for what it is—just a setback, not a verdict. I've had to overcome obstacles and let go of controlling the outcome of my story. I trust the universe always has my back and Source to light my path, even on the dark nights of my soul when light seems scarce. And I've come to appreciate the role of uLMS as an unrelenting teacher who has, although originally unwelcomed in my life, provided the greatest lesson of all— to keep living my now very richly fulfilling life with grit, one precious moment at a time.

Cheryl cultivated just shy of four decades of higher education teaching, program administration, curriculum development, curriculum assessment, and faculty development. She has joyfully supported and uplifted hundreds of college-level learners in their capstone/research projects at the baccalaureate to post-doc levels. She received numerous nominations for teaching excellence, having served students in medical schools, private teaching universities, colleges of health sciences, and more, working with 2-year students, 4-year undergraduates, as well as graduate students at the masters, doctoral, and post-doctoral levels.

For half of her academic career, she brought her teaching and administrative skillset to assessment and accreditation. She served as lead reviewer for the Accreditation Council for Education in Nutrition and Dietetics (ACEND®), the accreditation agency of the Academy of Nutrition and Dietetics, for 17 years.

Now retired, she is fiercely competitive during family game night, documents cherished moments with her two young grandchildren, and lives each day in the precious present moment.

Please scan the QR code to connect with this author.

Holly Breuer

I'm Always Ok

I believe everything happens for a reason. I also believe that if you do things for the right reasons, you'll be ok.

I'm always ok.

My story begins on March 3, 2023, because the events leading up to that day are covered by a non-disclosure agreement that, in the words of my lawyer, "was agreed upon by and beneficial to both parties." Point is, I woke up on March 3rd, owning a public accounting firm, which had fewer clients than employees, and I was weirdly calm. We outsourced ourselves to larger accounting firms and the trust department of a bank, and those fees helped keep the doors open. Metaphoric doors, of course.

The team had taken up residence at a client's office, taking over the lunchroom, a couple of offices, and anywhere else with a flat surface. There was no room for me, so I worked from home and drove to the office a couple of hours a day to help where I could. The team worked on card tables and folded chairs with stacks of boxes used as shelving and makeshift filing systems. And they were working hard, speed-typing on laptops I handed out to them from the trunk of my car in the parking lot of a restaurant we met at for lunch. I think the more they had to do that, the more worried they were getting, but I was the opposite. If we could get this much work done under these circumstances, there would be no stopping us when we had desks and chairs!

As word spread around the accounting community that we existed, I received several offers from prominent firms that wanted to absorb the team, but our team members were vocal that this was not what they wanted. I had made a promise to listen to them and follow through on the course of action voted for by the majority, so I turned down those offers. This wasn't always easy. At one point, I had just gotten a second round of investment money for the firm and said aloud in my kitchen, "Wow… we owe more on these investments than we do on our home mortgage." I looked over at my husband, whose body stiffened as he stood at the sink washing a pot. As he turned to face me, I said, "Is that scary to you?" "Yeah. You know, it really is," he said as he slowly let out a breath. I realized at that moment that there was a part of me that didn't think any of this was even real. Was it an out-of-body experience? Maybe, but I felt like I was on a course that included nine other peoples' lives and livelihoods. I agreed to do this, and they were counting on me, so what was the point in thinking too hard about it?

When I look back on my life, nothing was sending me in this direction. I met my ex-husband when I was far too young. It wasn't a good marriage, and by the time I was pregnant with our second child, he had moved on to someone else. In retrospect, it was probably the kindest thing he had ever done, but it most definitely didn't feel that way at the time. At 29 years old, I was a hairdresser, but not a particularly good one, so with no real marketable skills, I went back to college to finish a degree I started in my teens.

I decided I was going to work at a bank. I figured banker's hours were good, and it would be a profession that I could be proud to have. I enrolled and filled out the FAFSA paperwork to get a loan. I had to come up with the money to buy the books for my first semester, so I sold my engagement ring and went to the bookstore. I purchased the five huge textbooks I needed for my business classes and, as I drove home, had to pull over on the side of the road to cry. What the hell was I doing? I had always done well in school, but I hadn't been in a classroom in almost a decade. And it wasn't like I was following in somebody's footsteps. I had family members with varying numbers of completed college credit hours, but nobody finished the job. I come from a family used to back-breaking work. They're smart people, but opportunities to go to college weren't there.

My college education also came with strings attached. I was a single mom with two children and no money. Because my son was so young, daycare was paid for by the state while I was in class, the children were on Medicaid, and we received food stamps and $269 a month to live on. In exchange, the government was in my life. For the first semester, my professors graciously signed a weekly attendance sheet that I scanned and emailed to my social worker to prove I was where I said I'd be.

Ten years older than the other students, I sat in the front row of every class, read every textbook, and asked every question. That's all I could do. When the hard work paid off and I had an A in every class, I was no longer required to prove my attendance. After a couple of semesters, my finance degree advisor suggested I switch my major to accounting: "A CPA can do finance, but a finance professional can't be a CPA." What I knew about accounting was that it was the only class I dropped out of in high school. My teacher was Methuselah's older sister, who prided herself on forging her incredibly long teaching career on monotony and boredom. Looking forward to more accounting? I thought not but reminded myself that I was there for my children and my future, so if this advisor thought this was the best route, then I was prepared to get through it. Once in the class, though, I felt the opposite. Accounting was the one thing that made sense in my life at that time. If I did the calculations correctly, one piece would flow into another, and my accounts would balance when everything else in my life was in chaos. My homework made me calm and focused. The kids got to bed around 8 p.m. and I'd study until midnight, then wake up at 4 a.m. to get some more work done before they woke up at 6 or 7 a.m. To this day, when things are crazy around me, I try to lose myself in a spreadsheet: calculating, formatting, getting everything just right until my brain feels better. If you know, you know.

I pushed through to earn my MBA because there are college hour requirements for CPAs in Missouri that I hadn't hit, but I was getting antsy. It didn't matter that I was killing it in the classroom because I was back to reality off campus. I had survived figuring out how to make meals for the kids with the two-pound blocks of cheese allotted to me monthly from the WIC program. I budgeted myself by putting the cash from my government checks into marked envelopes and when an envelope was empty, we did without - be it clothes, shoes, school supplies, or gas for the car. I had an internal voice that told me this wasn't about me. This was temporary, and I was never going to live like this again. It can still be a little soul-crushing when a cashier holds up a TANF (Temporary Assistance for Needy Families) card to the crowded line at a busy grocery store and yells over at me, "Is this card for food stamps? Food stamps? Ma'am... food stamps?" The humiliation was real, but it was cushioned a little bit because I was doing this for my babies. If I had to walk through glass on my tongue for them, I would. I'd wear this humiliation as an honor. That internal voice was getting me through again, but I'd be lying if I didn't acknowledge that typing that story right now didn't just knock me back a bit again. Anyway, after going through that period of my life, jumping off a cliff into public accounting seemed easy, right? I mean, once you've been humiliated at the grocery checkout, what else can they do to you?

Turns out, banker's hours weren't in the cards. Fifteen-hour days? Check. Holidays? Nights? Weekends? Check. Check. Check. Public accounting is not for the faint of heart. The learning curve seems to get steeper the higher you get, nothing gets easier, and imposter syndrome is just part of the gig. It takes a special breed of masochist to thrive in this climate. But I love doing this job and, even more so, being around like-minded folks.

Public accounting is the only career path that allows me to be around these amazing people each day. The thing about being an accountant at the local widget factory is that I would want to talk about accounting, but everyone else would talk about widgets. Yuck! I worked my way up the ranks. I didn't have a resume with a top-tier business school, parents in the business, or friends that would be clients. What I have is a dogged belief that if someone else can do it, then I can, too.

I took that belief with me to this new chapter of my life as a small business owner. I mean, people start businesses all the time, right? So why couldn't I? I didn't know what the name of this new accounting firm would be, but I knew it wasn't going to be Breuer CPAs. This was a team, and I was going to be one of the players and maybe sometimes the coach. It was most definitely not going to be "my firm" with "my people." We settled on "Prosper" for the firm's name because it gave us a one-word focus. I wouldn't prosper unless the rest of the team did, and they wouldn't prosper unless our clients did, so that focus was outward, where it belongs. Hearing what types of work our accountants like to do is part of this. If someone enjoys reviewing ledgers but hates preparing tax returns, why would I make them prepare tax returns? That just never made sense to me.

My personal goal for that first year was to meet as many people as possible to get the Prosper name out there. I accepted *all* the invites – breakfast, lunch, drinks, Zoom, Teams, Google Meet, telephone, smoke signal. It didn't matter…I was there. A bit of a stretch for someone who is a natural introvert. Not one of those hide in the closet introverts, more one that lays on the ground in a fetal position after too much revelry. Oddly, though, I think I'm growing to enjoy the role. I've lost track of how many times I grudgingly made my way to a lunch meeting only to find myself having a tough time ending it because I was fascinated by the person across the table from me.

We finally got desks and chairs, too! After my husband, son, and I spent five months maneuvering around 100-pound, 6-foot boxes stacked up in my living room, family room, hallways, and any nook and cranny we could find, it was finally time to move into our very first office. We had team members, their spouses, and family members grab hammers, screwdrivers, and whatever tools were brought or were in the pink tool kit my Daddy gave me for Christmas years ago and built them on-site. The team got some pizza before they got there as trade for the hard labor. I was right, too, because that team is unstoppable! We've onboarded what should be an unbelievable number of clients in the last two years and have hired five more team members to help us keep up. We're far outpacing my original projections, so I think we're only going to be held back by our imagination. I guess I'll start loading up some more boxes to get ready for our next move. I don't know where it's going to take us, but it's going to be ok, right? I mean, people do this sort of thing all the time.

Holly Breuer is the Founder and President of Prosper CPAs, a public accounting firm based in Chesterfield, Missouri. With over 20 years of experience, she specializes in providing regulatory and operational consultation for privately held businesses, with expertise in strategic planning, M&A transactions, and compliance processes. Holly is dedicated to helping businesses optimize value and streamline operations to achieve long-term goals. She has built lasting client relationships, always prioritizing their success.

An active member of the Missouri Society of CPAs, Holly has served as the past Chair of both the Women's Initiative and Firm Leadership Committees. She is also a member of the American Institute of Certified Public Accountants.

Holly holds an MBA and a B.S. in Accountancy and has earned numerous awards, including Top Small Business Accountant by *St. Louis Small Business Monthly* in 2024, 2023, and 2022, and Top 50 Women Leaders of St. Louis in 2024.

Please scan the QR code to connect with this author.

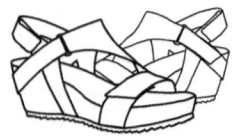

Beverly Jenkins

Lessons from Railroad Avenue

I can still smell the air on my favorite dirt road street, Railroad Avenue. It was always thick, with a quarter cup of dust mixed with a tablespoon of ditch dross, and a smidgen of freshly mowed grass. Railroad Avenue was and is my nostalgic childhood memory. It was the place I found my legs and my voice. It was my promised land.

It has become my fondest memory, not because of the street, but because of what the street represented as well as the "who" that centered me while living there. My grandmother stood about 5'6", maybe 5'7" if she had on her church shoes. She was the epitome of a classy woman with grace all her own. She was a woman of strength and character. I grew up in her home. The home was multi-generational. My mom lived there, my uncles lived there, and me. It was a most wonderful experience. I attribute all my humor and wisdom before my time to growing up with old people. Yes, I grew up in Poplar Bluff, Missouri, on Railroad Avenue, 1017 Railroad Avenue, to be exact.

It was just me. I was the baby, the only baby. The only child of my flower child, vivacious, drop-dead gorgeous mother. My grandmother, Mama Lee, had a real hand in raising me. Well, everyone in that house truly did, and for that I am grateful. Mama Lee, however, instilled some things that just stuck and have become a cornerstone to all the foundational tenets that I have learned to govern my life by.

Dust Always Settles

Railroad Avenue is a dirt rocky road still to this day. It spanned about a half mile long, and on a day without rain, it was the dustiest dust bowl of all time. My Mama Lee and I would go out to the porch to have a glass of tea and talk. She would talk to me as if I were the one and only human she could have a conversation with, even though I was just elementary school age. We talked about the trains across the track and watched often as they would barrel by so fast. We had a competition to count as many train cars as possible before we got to the caboose.

As we sat there sometimes in the smoldering heat, cars would speed by on the dirt rock road and kick up a dust storm something fierce. I was young, so the dust was fun to watch. It would kick up high in the sky and make a mess of everything in its path. We would sneeze relentlessly, but no matter how much dust the car stirred up, it would always eventually settle right back down to the ground from whence it came. Herein lies one of the earliest lessons I learned. Dust is dust. It has no real substance. It is light and airy, and without a catalyst, it is nothing dangerous really. However, it is annoying as a gnat on a spring day. It can cloud a beautiful landscape in seconds.

Dust does, however, parallel life's inconvenient moments. How many times in your life has "dust" clouded your vision, strangled your voice, choked the air from your lungs, and caused you to have to turn your head away? It is not unlike what happens when we encounter resistance or pain. What we must remember is that in the end, "the dust settles." Everything is still in the same place it was before. The dust only masked it. Eventually, it falls back down to the earth that it came from, and you will see the thing you held in your sights clearly again.

Avoiding the Ditch

Every good country road has a ditch, and boy, oh boy, did Railroad Avenue have the biggest, deepest ditches in town. May I also add, ditches that were full of delectable crawdads—I digress.

My grandmother's driveway was rocky as well, and for whatever reason on both sides of this "driveway" were two massive ditches. You had to drive with great precision to get into the driveway and most definitely had to be amazing at backing out. However, for those of us who lived on Railroad Avenue and had been down the pathway many times, navigating this space was like second nature. I watched my uncles pull in and out like professional stuntmen. It also always baffled me that our mailbox was a country mile away, around the corner, to be exact. However, now I realize it was most likely for the mailman's safety to avoid those ditches.

Occasionally, we would have a guest come to town. These were the people we would call "company." Mama Lee would say "Company is coming over." All that meant was to clean up the house right now. They would warn the company of the ditch, but the company always thought that they were the best driver in town and would never end up in a ditch. But guess what, they did every time.

Why did they fall in the ditch? Partly, because they did not heed the warning of those who had gone before them. They already knew the pitfalls and the lumps in the road, the false foundation that was on the right bend. They knew what it was like to drive on this road in the dark, when it was rainy, when it was muddy, when it was clear. They were the experts.

We all need guidance when we are in a quandary. It is wise to take counsel. It has never failed me in my life to ask for understanding from those that have trudged the path prior to me getting there. I have not asked anyone on my journey for insight or advice I was desperate for, which they did not willingly share.

Many who have fallen into proverbial ditches have done so because they felt they were too awesome a driver to need a guide to back out of a tight spot. After all, they have driven before. Yet, when we hit the ditch and there was no way out, we now need a different kind of expert—a tow truck.

There Is No Downtown in the Country

Every two weeks or so, Mama Lee and I would take a walk to what she called Uptown. I have no idea why she called it that. I never heard the term downtown until I moved to the big city. The walk was long toward uptown, and I didn't care how long the walk was as long as I was in her company. I knew I was finally off Railroad Avenue as my shoes made a new sound on the pavement. Click Clack, Click Clack. When we headed uptown, we always put on the best clothes, not to impress, but as a sign we were going to do business. How did I know this? Because Mama Lee would carry her pocketbook—that was the name she gave to purses. If my grandmother grabbed her pocketbook, that meant she meant business, and we'd be gone for a bit. She had clear intentions when we headed out on that walk. My only goal was to get some chiclet gum and possibly some sugar babies.

It is a weird thing to look back on my life and realize that these walks really taught me to look ahead and see that I could go anywhere I wanted. In hindsight, my sight was being trained to visualize up and not down. Please note, this is from the perspective of a grown woman now looking back on my life as a child and embracing the intersections that have brought me to investigate why I think the way I do. Why do I see up when most see down? Why do I see a way forward when most say there is no way forward? It is because my grandmother gave me no other option other than to walk toward UP-town.

The Land and The House

It was somewhere around 1940, and I was nowhere on the radar. My beautiful grandmother needed a place to raise her children, and her husband was off to war. The scene was bleak, and prospects were even bleaker. She did the impossible in the '40s as a black woman; she bought her own land and built her own home right on, yep, Railroad Avenue. I have no idea how she did this. All I know is I am the evidence it really happened because I am an eyewitness. I grew up right there on this land and in this house that was my home for almost eleven years.

What bravery. What triumph. What significance this is to my current life now. I had no idea what she had accomplished while I was living there. She never spoke of it. However, when I came of age and a healthy dose of curiosity, I realized she had done the impossible.

My grandmother had taught me with one fell swoop that anything, absolutely anything, is possible when you believe…and go to work to get it done. I would have never dreamed of even attempting to purchase a shopping plaza within my community had it not been for the journey to Railroad Avenue.

Railroad Avenue is probably not the dream home for anyone who is reading this. It is a dirt road that many avoid in this current day. Heck, most people avoided it back then, but it was my dream home. It was my happy place. It is the place my mind runs to when I am having a moment. It is the place I still dream about in my sleep and wake up rested.

I owe my grandmother so much. She was a life force all on her own. I spent my life sitting in front of the wood stove listening to her stories, and she listened to mine as well. 1017 Railroad Avenue and all that raised me there are responsible for me being the woman I am today. I am proud of her. She loves her family, her friends, her God, and even a stranger or two, but more importantly, the talks on the dusty porch of Railroad Avenue taught her to love herself and embrace all the complexities of who she is becoming and unbecoming.

Pastor Beverly Jenkins holds the esteemed position of Founder as well as President and CEO of Refuge and Restoration Nonprofit, where she spearheads the economic development initiative as the visionary of the redevelopment project known as "The R&R Marketplace." Additionally, she serves as Co-Founder of Refuge and Restoration Church.

As founder of Refuge and Restoration, Beverly assumes the critical responsibility of overseeing the execution of the R&R Marketplace, a multifaceted 20-million-dollar development project and community investment located in Dellwood, MO. She ensures the comprehensive execution of the project's overall construction, pillars (programming), hiring strategy, and leasing of all lease spaces.

Beverly's educational accomplishments include a Master's degree in Organizational Leadership and Management, along with several certifications and other milestone accomplishments. They include IFF's Stronger Nonprofit Initiative in collaboration with Chase Bank as well as a graduate alumnus of the extensive Goldman Sachs 10k Businesses Cohort.

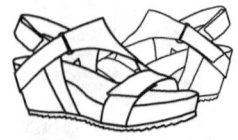

Daffney Moore, PhD

It Ain't Over

Hearing the words, "Your last day of employment will be December 31," was not how I intended to end 2022. I was terminated just as I was reaching new heights in my career. To add insult to injury, on January 6, 2023, there was a headline about my termination in the local newspaper. My face was plastered on the front page. My termination was now public. Immediately, the wave of phone calls, countless emails, and awkward public encounters began. I couldn't go to the grocery store without encountering someone who had heard about my misfortune and wanted to know what happened.

For many people, this experience would have resulted in withdrawing from the public eye and the community. I chose differently. On New Year's Eve, I decided that I would not retreat. As the final hours of 2022 approached, I checked into a hotel and celebrated with strangers in the hotel restaurant. When the clock struck midnight on December 31, 2022, I knew then that while my life had just taken a plot twist, I would not allow this situation to define me. I sure as hell was not going into hiding. I decided to seize control of the narrative. I had worked too hard and done right by the staff and the community for too many years to allow one moment to immobilize me. I embraced the unknown, held tight to my faith and God's hand, and started a new journey not defined by my job.

I Am Not My Job

Early on, I decided I would not allow this experience to dictate my future. I understood that most Black women do not have the luxury of not being resilient. Deciding not to let job loss define me was the first step toward resilience and personal empowerment. This new season was an opportunity for growth and healing. I would not succumb to despair. I needed to trust God's plan. This would not be easy, but it was necessary so I would not fall into hopelessness. I shifted my focus from loss to opportunity. This was an opportunity for development and self-discovery. My life and self-worth were not tied to a job and a title. While I took my time exploring new possibilities, I did my best to stay positive by engaging in activities that made me happy. But being unemployed made it difficult to enjoy some of my favorite pastimes. Luckily, I had planned and paid for two major trips, which I decided to keep.

Use Your Favorite Pastime to Get You Through

If you know me, you know I love sports. Sports have always played a crucial role in my life, serving as an escape and a way to relieve stress. While baseball was my first love, I eventually became an avid football fan, often traveling to games. So, what does a girl do after losing her job? She goes to the Super Bowl! I had always wanted to attend the Super Bowl, so I had planned a trip to attend the 2023 game. The Super Bowl and a series of pre-planned trips evolved into more than mere escapades; they provided the energy and excitement I needed at the time. These moments of enjoyment were essential to my reclamation of my spirit. Travel emerged as a therapeutic tool for me. From attending the men's and women's Final Four games to adventures in Toronto and Puerto Rico, each journey brought new perspectives and renewed strength. The experiences highlighted the importance of living fully, regardless of employment status, and affirmed my capabilities beyond professional confines.

Contribution and Connection: Volunteering

I had recently joined the board of directors for the Center of Creative Arts in St. Louis (COCA), and I never imagined the organization's impact on my life. This role provided another significant step in my journey. While not planning to lead any events that year, I was asked to be the COCAcabana board co-chair. COCAcabana is COCA's annual fundraiser, which draws over 500 business and community leaders annually. It showcases a festive evening of activities, artistic performances, appearances by special celebrity guests, and imaginative themes that embody COCA's creative essence. When asked to co-chair the fundraiser, I responded, "You know I don't have a job, right?" Despite my initial reservations and concerns, I accepted the role; this was COCA's only major fundraising event. This role gave me solace and purpose and integrated me into a supportive community that uplifted me during my most challenging times. COCA St. Louis became my second family. My co-chairs were amazing and welcomed me with open arms. We had fun, and there was such a powerful sense of love within the committee and organization that it deepened my commitment to the group. The most astonishing part of my volunteering was that, despite being unemployed and the organization having never done this, I suggested our goal to raise a million dollars for the group. We achieved our goal (thank God).

The Power of Support

I have never been one to ask for help unless it is necessary. Typically, I am the giver, the one others lean on, always eager to perform acts of kindness for friends and strangers—arranging spa days, trips, donations, and gifts. Yet, I learned during this ordeal to accept help, which was unfamiliar. My friends rose to the occasion, providing emotional support and tangible assistance, such as organizing trips and social events that uplifted my spirits. Their readiness to help reflected the strong bonds we had built over years of friendship.

Planning Your Next Steps

The journey from job loss to a renewed sense of purpose is not linear. It involves setbacks and victories, days of doubt, and moments of clarity. I needed to create a balanced, fulfilled blueprint that aligned with who I was and my future endeavors. I learned many lessons along the way and turned them into action steps to move forward with my life, which I want to share with you.

Lessons Learned & Key Action Steps

I Am Not Hiding: When the newspaper featured an article about me, going into hiding might have seemed the easiest thing to do. Instead, I chose visibility over retreating, which meant attending events where I often got the "surprised to see you here" look and the whispers. I was not going to allow anyone to narrate my story. My commitment to the community was unwavering, and I knew my worth. There was no need to hold my head down or indulge in self-pity. I had to trust God's process even though it was sometimes challenging. It presented an opportunity to set an example for others facing similar challenges, demonstrating that your job does not define you.

Key Action Steps:

- **Reflect on your immediate reaction:** It is expected to be emotional after a loss. Consider writing down your thoughts and feelings. Acknowledge what happened and challenge yourself to look beyond your current situation and move forward. This will help you stave off depression. However, it is important to seek help when you need it. I sought guidance from a therapist to make sure I was in a suitable mental space.

- **Choose your narrative:** While I did not like my name and information in the newspaper, I did not allow it to be a defining moment. People lose jobs all the time. Decide how you want to respond to your challenges. Will they define you, or will you author your own story?

Navigating Economic Uncertainty: Because I am an opinionated Black woman and very few women are in my field, I knew it might take some time to land a new position. So, I called my financial advisor to discuss and review my budget and investments to understand my finances better. Then, I contacted a former part-time employer to inquire about openings.

Key Action Steps:

- **Financial Prudence:** The financial impact of a job loss is significant but not insurmountable. I was unemployed for a year after that loss, but because I had been diligent with saving, I had a buffer and a clear plan for my finances.
- **Talk to Your Creditors:** I proactively communicated with creditors. I called creditors to inform them of my unemployment. To my surprise, when I contacted the mortgage company, they had multiple programs that allowed me to defer payments. This allowed me to focus on paying other bills.

Embrace the Season You Are In: When catapulted into my new season, I permitted myself to venture outside my professional identity and enjoy my time off. I immersed myself in being a tourist in my own city, picked up new skills, and indulged in periods of leisure and soul-searching. The time off allowed me to travel and gave me precious moments with my mom, which I cherished.

Key Action Steps:

- **Cultivate New Passions**: What are you interested in? I compiled a list of interests and hobbies I wanted to explore but never had the time. I engaged in new interests. Whether painting, writing, or running, a new season is the perfect time to embrace these interests.

- **Embark on a Journey**: Plan a getaway—no matter how modest the distance—just for you. A new environment can do wonders to help you heal, give you a fresh perspective, spark creativity, and gain fresh insights into your life.

The Power of Giving Back: Acts of kindness have a way of returning to us. I found that the more I gave, the more I received—not just in material form but in love, appreciation, and support. Engaging in community service provided a sense of purpose and joy. It connected me with people who inspired and uplifted me, reinforcing that I was not alone on this journey.

Key Action Steps:

- **Volunteer:** Find a cause that resonates with you and give your time. If you are unfamiliar with the organization, I suggest starting small. I had a great time volunteering, making an impact in the community, and connecting with others.
- **Be consistent:** Make giving back a regular part of your life. I had a blast volunteering with COCA St. Louis. They reminded me of my "why," which is serving the community and giving back to young people. It kept me busy, gave me a purpose and a focus, and allowed me to do something I enjoy.

Strategize and Move Forward: There comes a time when you must move forward and begin crafting the next chapter of your life. It's imperative to outline goals and create a plan to achieve them. Make sure your goals align with your future aspirations, identity, and core values.

Key Action Steps:

- **Set realistic goals:** What do you want to achieve in the next year? Break it down into actionable steps. My goal was to find a job that matched my non-negotiables, fit my personality, and respected my authenticity.

- **Embrace new opportunities:** Growth often comes from unexpected places. While I worked in economic development, I worked more on the administrative side. My new employer allowed me to do more real estate and project management.

This season of my life, marked by an unexpected job loss, became a profound lesson in resilience, authenticity, self-discovery, and the importance of community. Each moment taught me more about myself and the kind of life I wanted to live. From setting boundaries to exploring new opportunities, I discovered my value did not diminish because of professional setbacks. Instead, these experiences carved paths to deeper relationships, richer experiences, and intentional living.

Dr. Daffney Moore is a visionary leader, an advocate, and a relationship-builder, distinguished by her work in economic development within the St. Louis region. As one of the few Black women executives in her field, she excels in revitalizing communities through innovative solutions.

Currently, Dr. Moore is the Senior Director of Economic Development at Beyond Housing. Her expertise extends to academia as an adjunct instructor at Harris-Stowe State University, a role she has passionately held for seventeen years. In her previous positions, she has served as Chief of Staff, City Manager, and City Administrator.

Beyond her professional endeavors, Dr. Moore is deeply committed to civic engagement. She actively "opens doors" through her roles on several boards locally and nationally. Her dedication is pivotal in fostering community growth and enhancing the quality of life for others.

Dr. Moore's leadership and advocacy underline her commitment to driving significant social and economic change.

Please scan the QR code to connect with this author.

Brandi Jo Zirkelbach

The Power of Connection

Do you know the power of connection? Each time you come in communication with someone, you have a chance to make a connection that could potentially shape you or the other person's life—the ability to change their mood, the course of their day, the intention behind the now, and many other things.

Meet Corey. Corey is the FedEx delivery guy in my neighborhood. Long shifts are inevitable, and you see him every day without fail, always with a smile. One morning, I was waiting for something incredibly special (my competition suit prototype) at my home and it came earlier than expected! I just so happened to be meal prepping for the next few days and prepared him food to go. "Why?" you ask. When the truck pulled up, I knew exactly what was arriving, and I ran outside so excited. He immediately asked what was in the package and then proceeded to ask about my athletic career and if he could follow along in my progress.

His next question was, "What else do you do as your profession?" I learned his name and ran inside to prepare him a boxed lunch. He had no idea how important it was to me that he took the time out of his super demanding route to get to know me, and I had to immediately add value the best way I knew how. Now, we run into each other everywhere—he delivers to my office, my home, the title company, the bank, the nail shop, and so on. We chat and learn something new about one another every trip! I inspire him to take better care of his body and mind, and he inspires me to always smile and stay true to my values in terms of customer service and care. That is the power of connection.

About three years ago, I came to realize that I could no longer continue the way I had been in my business and started to plan for the next growth phase. I had been in real estate long enough to understand what I was lacking and where I wanted to go. All my goals set before then had been satisfied, but I was tired and overwhelmed. How do you exceed your own expectations if you are burning your candle at both ends? How long is that sustainable? The next step was to start building systems and design a business plan that fit where I wanted to be in one year, three years, five years, and ten years, with the understanding that I would have to sacrifice my own earning potential to grow through sharing, coaching, and cultivating culture.

Do you ever have visions of how you want things to pan out? I have been a dreamer, a planner, a goal-setter, and a master connector of sorts for as long as I can remember. And let me tell you, this lady was ready for the next phase! Along the way, I had someone offer me $50,000 as an advance and ask me if that would help me grow. "Well, yeah," but I did not want more debt. They thought it could get me where I was going faster, but hasty decisions—especially financial ones—and I do not get along. So, I sat and thought about what I really wanted. And the answer was "time."

How does someone create time? What does that even mean? You don't take the loan, but you want time? Most people would've taken it and vacationed someplace exotic as a gift they thought was well deserved. Or dumped it in a small investment in hopes of big returns! Not me; I knew I was going to have to take big risks.

Back to my definition of buying time...I wanted time to live outside of my career. BJZRealty LLC was founded in 2015, and I have worked no less than seventy hours a week since then. Before that, in another life, I had worked more than seventy hours—three jobs, nights, weekends, holidays, and everything in between. There was a time when it had been fourteen years since I had even a three- or four-day vacation. This is not me bragging or complaining; I want to bring you to my headspace. The only way to buy yourself time in the career of real estate is to build a team or to scale back. If you knew your girl, scaling back is not in my genetic makeup! So, the systems and models would become phase one.

When I first started my career in real estate, I knew that absorbing as much as I could from those before me was the way. The only way. The company I chose advertised heavily about their educational training and culture, and I was incredibly drawn to that. You mean to tell me that I can learn all there is to know about real estate in a super-rich, diverse, and supporting culture? I am in! And I did. Day in and day out, I would leave work at 3 or 4 a.m., get the kids off to school, head to the office for class, and rinse and repeat every day. It was important to me to continue to immerse myself in as much education and culture as I could. Understanding the methodologies of real estate sales, contracts, law, ethics, and care was so interesting to me. I began to understand that I could practice retail sales on a larger scale and actually change people's lives.

There was a saying I learned while attending class back then: "Live a life worth living and a legacy worth leaving," meaning, pursue a life with meaning and sustenance, make choices that will affect you and the others around you positively, and leave while continuing to care for and inspire. That stuck with me and became part of my business plan. I wanted to create a real team culture built on those values, educating and delivering with intention, creating goals that align with a positive legacy. For me, it is about impacting others around me, including family, friends, colleagues, and clients alike. We aren't talking about financial legacy; we are providing opportunities for people I otherwise had to create for myself.

While focusing on finding the time, actively living a fulfilling lifestyle, and taking care of my family, how did I reach these goals in business? By bringing others around as an extension of me. It isn't a perfect science, but through teaching life skills, personal development techniques, standards of service, and culture, you can accomplish beautiful things if you show people how to love and care for themselves, demonstrate some account-ability, and support them fully. It may take some time, but they become strong, confident, capable people.

I love what I do with every fiber of my being and had developed a business that gifted me the name "St. Louis Concierge of Real Estate." You don't get that by being lackadaisical. It comes from sheer grit, discipline, and standards of business. You must pay attention to detail, have advanced troubleshooting skills, understand time management, and have a large network of support. Helping people and using my maternal instincts to practice care at the highest level is my love language. Acts of service, gift giving, and the ability to work through even the toughest issues with creativity and grace are my strengths. It is absolutely amazing to be able to share these experiences and will a library of knowledge to others. I treat my teammates like family. I want to give them more opportunities, show them how to manage stress, and help them find a work-life balance by supporting them through mentoring, training, and all the tools they need to get off to a great start.

Buying myself time, creating opportunities for others, cultivating my team, building a rich culture, and homing in on and improving coaching skills have all now become a new set of goals.

While I am proud to know I am a self-made woman, I didn't get here alone. Yes, I am a single mother who raised two kids and a grandchild with no man in the house or direct maternal support. I have never been married and am one hundred percent the sole provider of my household. But no, I did not do this alone.

Over the course of my working career, I have been in customer service in some capacity for thirty years. And within that time, I have become a master connector. You want to understand the power of connection? Before I started to build a team, I had hosted a holiday client appreciation event and started to introduce my clients to my new agents, transaction coordinator, and cleaning technicians. The feedback was that they always thought I had a team and couldn't understand how I accomplished that level of service on my own. I have never been on my own. I learned at a very young age that there is someone for everyone, and that translates into work, networking, relationship building, and client relations. Learning how to form relationships and connect one person's priorities, needs, and wants into someone else's profession and vice versa makes a team. So, to all the servers, bartenders, drivers, plumbers, carpenters, investors, designers, attorneys, mentors, and more of the world, thank you! You allowed me to learn about your business, what your goals are, your strengths and needs, and how to refer you to the next one! What's so great is that now we can help facilitate the needs of my clients and yours as a collective effort. I have succeeded at building a collective culture through the power of connection.

Brandi Jo Zirkelbach is the owner of BJZRealty LLC, BJZ Real Estate Collective, and Concierge Cleaning Services LLC,

Originally from Evansville, Indiana, she moved to St. Louis, Missouri, in 2006. Her career before real estate was in customer service. Restaurants, clubs and bars, and hotels and hospitality are where she picked up on how to really understand people's needs and how to serve them both with care and intention. St. Louis was like a little big city to her! There are so many people to meet, but primarily small business owners and entrepreneurs. She was enchanted by it!

She soon became immersed in St. Louis culture and everything the city had to offer. So much so that she wanted to contribute to the community as well. So, in 2014, she began the process of becoming a realtor. For her, it was the perfect mix of art, service, and business. She has raised two children and is a lover of art, music, and anything outdoors. She is also a professional women's physique competitor in the IFBB Professional League and travels the states in hopes of earning her Olympia qualification.

Please scan the QR code to connect with this author.

Carmen Fronczak

The Search

At age 52, I have had five lives. Notice I don't use the word "chapters," but I use "lives." Every one of them leads me to the next one. Some might view multiple lives as failure, but I view it as being blessed to be the Carmen I am today. Some lives were easier and some harder, and then being left with only the cherished pieces is beautiful. Would I make each of these decisions over again? Yes, because any change in my history would change where I am and who I am today.

As I reflect on each person, each job, and every move, they all served a purpose during that time of my search. God placed them perfectly in the right place at the right time for some reason. I don't have any regrets, but I do wish I would have realized the value of family, time, and others' hearts much, much sooner. Especially the part about others' hearts. I walked away from many people who gave me the world and their entire heart.

Where do I begin? I grew up in multiple small Missouri towns, but mostly Farmington and Arnold, Missouri. In Farmington, we grew up on a farm in the country. It was awesome to grow up and know how to drive a tractor, ride a dirt bike, fish, boat, and ski. My dad, who I would have considered my hero, died from alcoholism when I was age 13. His disease and death are two of the driving factors that defined my life choices.

While my childhood inspired me, it had some struggles, too, but I was surrounded by the best mom, sisters, and friends a person could ask for. I would argue I had the most possible fun every day. I did it all.

My five adult lives would be defined around the guy in my life at that time of my search. They would read something like Peter, Ken, Doug #1, Doug #2, and Ted. I was always organizing my life around a guy. I hadn't realized yet that my life needed to be centered around me instead of another person. I couldn't find contentment. I couldn't sit still long enough to enjoy what I had. I was too busy creating a life that would fit into someone else's life. Then bam! There was a moment in my 30s when the lightbulb went off, and I started to focus on myself. That sounds selfish, but I don't mean it that way. For once, I wanted my own success more than I wanted someone's last name.

Let me give you a snapshot of the words that come to mind with each of these five lives:

- Peter – Missouri Baptist, snowboarding, Soulard, Jeeps, hippie, lake, friends, nursing school, and our amazing daughter Isabel.

- Ken – True Blue, the first person to believe in me, Medical West, spoiled, special, and will always be there.

- Doug #1 – Maui, Rhode Island, Aspen, Vail, travel and surf the world, and healthy and gorgeous.

- Doug #2 – My rock, Twisters, best extra dad ever, camper, Ocean City, best influence, and our amazing son Archer.

- Ted – Magnets, lake, chemistry, Vegas, Mexico, fun, running, crazy kid crew together, BABY, the most fun I have ever had, and the first person I couldn't walk away from.

All these people and experiences make me who I am. I was always searching. The tattoo on my left ankle is a surfing symbol that means "the search." It really means searching for the best wave ever, but to me, it was the search I was always on. I always thought there must be more. Why am I anxious and not settled?

Through the years, I have been a registered nurse, director of marketing, blueberry farmer, mom, bar owner, vintage clothing designer, Tiffany diamond sales specialist, real estate broker, healthcare business development vice president, and more. I'm not going to lie, I love that I did all these things, but I was never 100 percent in on any one of them. Just like the guys in my life, I was moving on to the next job or title, credentials, or degree. Maybe I should be happy about it…who has done all these things?

As a nurse in her 30s, I decided to go back to school and get my bachelor's degree in business and then a master's degree in health informatics. I also began a long journey to be the best in my field of senior living. I am confident enough to say that I am there. I have the best job in the world now. I am the chief revenue officer of Friendship Village Senior Services and the executive director for Friendship Village Chesterfield. I get to work alongside an amazing team and help lead the efforts to make this the best place to work and live. I am living my best work life, and my professional dreams are coming true. I love what I do!

The best part about my job is working with my team and our employees and trying to coach and motivate each one of them to find their life. What do they want their story to be? More importantly, how can I help and support them? This may be big or small. My life experiences have allowed me the opportunity to feel in tune with any type of employee at any level. My driving force at work is to make each employee feel their worth and importance. I thrive on this since I once struggled with it so much.

I may have swung the pendulum too far, though. My work-life balance is out of order. I put more energy, care, and time into work than I do my family. I know I can have it all. I just have to find the right balance.

I need to get back to living! I need to get back to giving my family the time it deserves, including my new granddaughter, Charlotte. I am burning the candle at too many ends. I work a lot and try to squeeze in three board of director roles, volunteering, and more. My son is traveling for hockey, and I often feel there isn't enough of me to go around. My marriage is often sacrificed for all these other things.

I know I will find balance. I will do it because I always find a way. I have the grit to keep going and to be better. The opportunity to write a chapter in this book with these other amazing authors is incredible, but I was too busy to find the time to do it. It was important to me; I just didn't have the capacity.

The reason it was important is that I do want my story to be told for other women out there who might be searching to create their life around a certain person. If you keep feeling unsettled, then I really would love to offer my advice and say, "Find yourself." That doesn't mean what I did is the right way to do it. Not everyone will want a career, but you can find out what you want and *go for it*. For me, it was my career. It gave me the self-worth and purpose I had sought for decades.

I'm not done yet. I want to do so much more and dream of more. I want to do more in my career and, more importantly, in my roles as mom, wife, and Granny C. The good news now is that I can stand on my own two feet. I have grown in ways I never knew were possible. I am happy with me. This will be the fuel to help me get my work-life balance back in place. This will be the fuel that ultimately leads me to my next chapter in this life. Notice, I didn't say another life. That's because I just want my next, best chapter with Ted and our family.

I am proud of who I am and where I came from. I am proud of the journey that I've been on. The extra bonus of writing this is it makes me even more vulnerable with those I lead. I believe vulnerability is one of the best leadership qualities of amazing leaders.

So, I ask you, what life will you search to live? Are you there, or will you get there? The good news for each of us is we are never alone because God has uniquely created each of us and already knows what life we will live. I wish you luck on your search. Remember, some lives are easier and some harder, and then being left with only the cherished pieces is beautiful.

Carmen is the chief revenue officer at Friendship Village Senior Services and is the executive director for Friendship Village Chesterfield. She is passionate about being a part of seniors' lives and strives to make a difference by delivering operational excellence. She brings 25-plus years of experience in healthcare business development, holds a bachelor's degree in business administration, a master's degree in health informatics, and is a registered nurse. Her expertise includes sales and marketing, strategic planning, start-up operations, and sales team management for independent living, assisted living, skilled nursing, and home health care. Since joining the company in 2013, Carmen has been integral in facilitating business growth.

Carmen's ongoing volunteer work has become a defining characteristic for her. She currently serves on the boards of LeadingAge Missouri and the Independence Center and is also the board chair of Titan 100 St. Louis.

Carmen is married to her husband Ted, and together they have four children, a son-in-law, and one granddaughter. Carmen's hobbies include spending time at the lake, wake surfing, snowboarding, and traveling to warm destinations. Her best days are when she can have her entire family together in one spot.

Tangela Williams

Playing for Keeps

Many people have asked me why I quit teaching. I give them a variety of answers, ranging from stress-related illness to just not being fun anymore. Some of my answers are more interesting than others, but all of them have a nugget of truth within them. The bottom line was I didn't enjoy it anymore, and it was killing me inside. One of the happiest days I spent in the classroom toward the end of my tenure was the April day that I told my supervisor that I would not be returning for the next school year.

The freedom I felt for the remainder of that semester was exhilarating. I was able to teach the way that I wanted to and have some fun with the students. Without the burden of administrative evaluations and expectations, teaching regained a glimmer of the glow that I had imagined for the rest of my working career.

However, the specter of summer loomed, and I didn't have a plan—no job lined up and a limited amount of savings to work with until something else came along. I knew that traditional teaching was no longer for me. There are a lot of problems present in the educational system that get filtered down to the teachers. It isn't fair, and I no longer wanted to carry that burden.

This left me with a small identity crisis. I had been working in classrooms since 2006. I'd earned my master's degree in special education and was licensed to teach in three states. I was supposed to teach for the rest of my working days. Now, I was directionless and empty. My mental health was beginning to deteriorate, and I was a pile of self-shame and annoyance.

Whenever real life gets too much for me, I run to the world of video games for solace. As an elder millennial, the video gaming industry in the United States grew up at the same time as I did. I was born in the spring of 1983, and the Mario Bros. arcade cabinet hit the streets at the same time. I have fond memories of trying to shoot the ducks with the orange and gray zapper on a black and white television in my uncle's house as a little girl.

I owned various consoles over the course of my life, from the Sega Genesis to the Dreamcast, from the Nintendo Game Boy to, most recently, the Nintendo Switch. Gaming has been a huge part of my life and a blessing to me in my times of need.

While I was wallowing in self-pity that summer, I played a lot of games. Mostly to have something to kill time but also as a distraction between hunting for jobs and filling out countless applications.

The weeks slowly became months, and my unemployment stretched on. My days became an endless cycle of job hunting and playing video games. It eventually got to the point that the two became eerily similar in my mind.

For starters, I was looking for a job. I didn't have any direction for my job hunt. To that end, I was using the same résumé I'd always used, just slightly updated with a more recent work history. I was also firing off random applications into the ether.

In gaming, one could call this method "button mashing." The world of fighting games hosts a variety of titles with memorable characters. For example, Chun-Li from the Street Fighter video game series. Any gamer that's very good at using Chun-Li as a fighter understands her moveset, or the buttons and combinations of buttons you must push to make the character kick and punch the way you want.

Advanced gamers can spot a button masher a mile away. There's no technique in the character's movements. The player is trying anything, and the character is flopping around all willy-nilly. Button mashers are easily exploitable and are generally viewed as a waste of time in competitive gaming communities.

It's the same thing in the career-hunting world. Recruiters can take one glance at a poorly constructed résumé or a sloppy application and toss it straight into the reject pile. When there is no polish or technique, you'll have no chance to show off what you could offer a company. The button mashing strategy isn't very effective.

In my personal attempts to overcome button mashing in games, I looked at a lot of videos to learn the best ways to play. Additionally, I had to practice. If you want any degree of high-level success, you have to work those fingers and thumbs. I got sick of looking at screens, but I certainly improved my gameplay performance.

The same principle applies elsewhere. I read a few essays and blog posts on better résumé writing to learn how to make them look more appealing and to tell better stories to recruiters. I also learned to tailor my résumés for the position I was applying for. Going through this process made me write a lot of résumés. It was frustrating, and I definitely got annoyed with it, but I did earn some success. My research garnered me a few interviews but no job offers. Back to the gaming console.

Many times, in video games, players will come up against unbeatable opponents or unconquerable quests. During those times, gamers can turn to a walkthrough for a guide on how to get past the tricky parts and successfully complete the game. These walkthroughs range from giving the player helpful hints to giving explicit instructions on how to achieve victory. Gamers do not always want to resort to the use of a walkthrough, but they are useful resources if the help is desired.

The same thing exists while job hunting. There are lots of workshops, books, and videos out there designed to help you clarify your goals, discover your desired career path, and obtain the career of your dreams. I needed clarity in my job hunt. I was applying for jobs that didn't align with my personal values, and I didn't feel drawn to their missions.

While on my journey of discovery, I improved a few more of my job-hunting techniques as well. Tricks like using keywords to get past A.I. filters greatly improved my responses to my job applications, and I scored a lot more interviews.

The interviews went fine, or so I thought, but I wasn't being called back to continue with the interview process. Granted, I had been employed in one place for a long time. My interviewing skills were probably a little bit rusty, but I didn't imagine that they were that bad. Apparently, I was wrong.

In a way, I had passed level one, but I had gotten stuck at level two. In our gaming analogy, things had gotten harder, and I was struggling. The opponents were a bit different, and I didn't have a great strategy for overcoming the challenge. I had to go back to the walkthrough to learn more helpful strategies.

I needed to use what I had previously learned in my research and expand a bit further. I discovered the value of having practice interviews. A lot of people tend to get uncomfortably nervous during interviews, and I was one of them. A person could be the most qualified candidate but can knock themselves out of the running by freezing up during the interview. It can be a huge blow to your confidence, but it can be overcome. By doing practice interviews, you can become extremely comfortable with the process. It may even become a matter of muscle memory. Job interviews can become as natural as breathing with the proper preparation.

I believe I reached this stage. With enough hard work, dedication, and perseverance, I landed a wonderful career with a company I believe in. The process was long and taxing. There were times when I believed that I would never get another job. I was afraid that I'd made the wrong decision for myself, and I would have to go crawling back to the classroom with my tail between my legs.

I could have given up at any point. I could have stayed angry and frustrated with the entire process and thrown in the towel. I could have easily succumbed to my self-doubt and taken another path. There have been times I've given up on certain games for a time. Throwing my controller away in anger, I would turn things off, curse, and fume. However, with all the skills I learned from video games over the years, I had the inner strength to stay the course and reach my goals.

I know the comparison between job hunting and gaming is different, but you know what they say: "You can't win a game if you don't play."

Tangela Williams-Spann is a social worker, writer, mother, favorite auntie to many, and mental health advocate. She enjoys using her unique voice to share the experiences of Black Women and Femmes in America. Tangela is the author of two books, *Sad, Black, and Fat: Musings from the Intersection* (2021) and *Brazen, Black, and Free: Further Musings from the Intersection* (2024). Her passion for teaching and learning has allowed her to obtain degrees in sociology and special education. When not looking for effective self-care strategies, she enjoys gardening, gaming, and crochet.

Please scan the QR code to connect with this author.

Nadine L. Kouba, PhD, PCC

Poster Girl—The Power of Networking

Today, I often refer to myself as the "Poster Girl" for all the mergers, acquisitions, and downsizings that occurred in St. Louis in the 1990s-2000s. Training and development, like Human Resources and Finance, are in every business. However, when financial times get tough, training resources are often the first to be sacrificed. Over the years, my grit has been tested as my positions have been downsized.

As a professional, I knew I was responsible for my professional development. While an employer might assist, the responsibility was mine. Therefore, in 1986, I joined two professional organizations that focused on training and development (The American Society for Training and Development) and organizational development (The Organizational Development Network). Both had local St. Louis chapters where I could attend programs, meet other professionals in my field, and become involved in committee work and board leadership. Several of the relationships I developed then remain as strong as ever today.

At the time, I never realized how important networking and the relationships that resulted would be for me and my career.

From early in my childhood, I knew I wanted to be a teacher. I first earned a bachelor's in secondary education with a major in English. Once

I completed my student teaching experience, I knew I would be better matched working with college-level students rather than secondary school-level students. With that in mind, I promptly pursued my master's degree in College Student Personnel. My intention was to work as a college administrator in higher education. Unfortunately, when I graduated with my master's, college enrollments dipped, and junior-level administrators were let go. I found myself competing for entry-level college adminis-trator positions with people who had anywhere from one to three years of college experience competing for the same entry-level positions.

I was forced to fall back on my undergraduate teaching degree and pursue high school English teaching positions. Thus, I taught high school English for two years for the Cleveland Public Schools. At the end of two years, I knew I was right about working with college-level students. I immediately started applying for college administrator positions and found a Residence Hall Director position with S.U.N.Y. Stony Brook. After two years at Stony Brook, I discovered I was a Midwesterner at heart. My parents retired and moved from Cleveland, Ohio, to Columbia, Illinois, so they could be a few minutes from my sister and their one and only grandchild in St. Louis. They moved my grandmother with them. Here I was, sitting in the middle of Long Island, wanting to move back to the Midwest. And my parents moved another ten hours further west! That caused me to look for university positions closer to St. Louis.

On my summer break from S.U.N.Y. Stony Brook, I visited my parents, who had relocated to Columbia, Illinois. If you've ever had that bad dream of your parents moving away and not knowing where they are, I lived it! Of course, they gave me their new address, but I had to use a map to get there. Cell phones and Google Maps didn't exist in the late 1970s.

Fortunately, I found a job as an Associate Director of Student Affairs with Parks College of St. Louis University, putting me within twenty minutes of my parents, grandmother, and sister's family. During my five-year tenure as a college administrator, I dealt with a flood, a fire, two student deaths, two students manifesting schizophrenia, assorted fights, numerous emotional crises, and a major snowstorm that prevented college employees from getting to the campus, causing my student residence life staff and I to prepare meals in the cafeteria for the dormitory residents. I was also completing my doctoral classes and beginning work on my dissertation. This left me exhausted after being on call 24 hours a day, seven days a week, and I left higher education to complete my dissertation and recover from burnout.

While I completed writing my dissertation, I decided to parlay my education, teaching experience, and management experience and apply for management training positions in business. Thus, my journey as a learning and development professional began, and memberships in my professional organizations started.

My first position was with The Jewish Hospital at Washington University Medical Center. I started as an instructor delivering management training programs. I was then promoted to Supervisor of Instruction with three direct reports. While at the hospital, I joined the St. Louis Chapter of the American Society of Training and Development (ASTD), now known as ATD (Association for Talent Development). ASTD held annual conferences for its members, and in 1986, the conference was held in St. Louis. Joining the Volunteer Committee allowed me to work with about eight other chapter members to establish the roles and responsibilities of conference volunteers.

About a year after the conference, one of my Volunteer Committee members called to recruit me to Union Electric Company (now known as Ameren). The job was not advertised publicly; instead, the company used a private recruiting process. Fortunately, I worked with one of the people recruiting for the position during the ASTD Conference, who knew my experience and work ethic. Networking paid off as I secured a new position that allowed me to grow and develop professionally and earn more income than in my previous position.

After four years at Union Electric, the Human Resources Vice President decided we would not update or initiate any new leadership training. I didn't see myself continuing to facilitate the same programs repeatedly without burning out. I noticed a job listing in my ASTD Chapter's newsletter and decided to apply.

Due to my managerial experience, training, and development experience, I landed the ASTD-advertised Director of Staff Development position with Correctional Medical Systems. Correctional Medical Systems implements contract healthcare in state and county prisons and jails. The new managers of those healthcare units started their new positions by attending a training program on managing a correctional facility healthcare unit, which reported to me. Thus, I have visited prisons and jails in nine states to understand the environment and needs of a correctional healthcare facility. One year, the company lost two state contracts and had to tighten the budget. My position was eliminated in October, and I was downsized.

In 1993, the economy tightened, and there were few open positions. I married in May 1993 so I could take advantage of my husband's health insurance when I was downsized. However, I earned the larger income of the two of us and needed to find a job. I turned to my ASTD colleagues for assistance in finding a new position. To my everlasting gratitude, one of my colleagues worked for Maritz Performance Improvement Company. Maritz had the largest custom design training company in the nation for the Fortune 100. My colleague knew the training division needed a contract Project Manager for a newly acquired contract. She carried my resume to the hiring managers. When my first contract was completed,

I continued to work as a contract designer and writer on several more projects. During this phase, my husband's company was sold. He stayed on for about a year, helping to close the plant. However, securing a full-time job became my priority as we needed healthcare benefits.

A Training Manager position opened in the Maritz Training Division. I was offered the position based on my work record as a contractor. I enjoyed working directly with clients in the Training Manager role but was less than satisfied. While I enjoyed developing programs, my real satisfaction came from seeing a program implemented and observing the results. As the Training team, we created and handed the programs to the client. Often, I never learned whether the program had achieved its intended goals.

The Director of Learning Systems position opened at the Maritz Travel Company. I applied and was selected. The Director position allowed me to work internally and see the full cycle of a program or initiative. While at the Travel Company, I joined the St. Louis Organization Development Network to pursue my interest in organization development. Too often, people thought training was the answer to non-performance rather than looking at the organization's structure or processes that might be causing the non-performance. My career goals were beginning to shift toward organizational development.

While at the Travel Company, I was contacted by a colleague who belonged to both the St. Louis ASTD Chapter and the St. Louis OD Network. She was recruiting for an OD/Training Manager position at her company. After discussing the position with her, I discovered it was the ideal combination of leadership development and organization development consulting. I applied to begin a new direction in my career, leveraging learning and development and adding in organization development consulting.

The position of Manager of Organization Development, then Director of Organization Development with Mallinckrodt, was exactly what I sought.

I also worked for my best boss and had great colleagues. Unfortunately, Tyco purchased Mallinckrodt. I, among many others, was downsized. While I was with Mallinckrodt, my husband had several health issues crop up and needed to take early retirement. We only had his Social Security income and the severance package I was given. My severance package quickly ate through our regular expenses and the massive COBRA Healthcare bill. I actively used the outplacement service I was given to find a new position.

I was fortunate to land a Director of Organization Development position with the Famous Barr division of the May Company. I enjoyed the employee discount and worked with many wonderful people. After five years with Famous Barr/May Company, Macy's purchased the May Company and all its divisions. Due to the acquisition, over 2,500 people were downsized in St. Louis, and I found myself on the job market once again!

Again, I received a severance package and outplacement services, and a new job search began. With all the downsizing happening in St. Louis, many people were seeking employment, with few available positions. Once more, I watched my severance package dwindle as I pursued my job search. A woman in my outplacement group landed a job in HR at GKN Aerospace. She told me that GKN had an open Talent Development Manager position in North America. It was up my alley, so I applied.

GKN allowed me to develop my talent development skills further. GKN was a British-owned subcontractor for major aerospace manufacturers. It created various airplane parts (windows, engines, seat tracks) for domestic and military aircraft. Unfortunately, when Boeing stopped accepting products from its subcontractors for the 787 Dreamliner, GKN had to tighten its budget. I found myself downsized once again.

The job market was again very tight. Since I'd only been with GKN for about two years, there wasn't a severance package, and I was on my own to maintain COBRA coverage and provide an income. My best boss from Mallinckrodt had moved to Emerson and ran the Emerson Learning Center. I checked with him to see if he knew of any positions or contract work I might pursue. It turned out that he needed someone to write a specific program, and he contracted with me to write it. Then, he needed a facilitator to travel and deliver a learning program in which I was certified. My connection to him provided me with contract work that let me earn an income while I pursued a full-time job.

A former colleague from Mallinckrodt had started her own business but also worked as a contract facilitator at the Boeing Leadership Center. She knew I was seeking a full-time position and told me about one at Boeing. I applied online for the Program Manager position. She also hand-carried my resume to the hiring manager and gave him a personal reference about the quality of my work. I worked for Boeing at the Leadership Center for seven years, then retired and started my part-time executive coaching business in 2018.

Once again, the relationships I built through networking paid off. One colleague connected me to a company that provides contract coaching to the federal government. I've worked with that company as a contract coach for several years. Another colleague connected me with a British consulting firm that hired me as a contract coach to coach executives in multiple international companies and their teams. A different colleague connected me with two universities, where I coach executives in an executive MBA program for one and in specially designed leadership programs for another.

In the era of downsizing that I experienced in my career, it certainly took some grit to maneuver through the ups and downs. I would not have succeeded without taking control of my development and networking with others. Building those relationships required partnering with others when they needed advice, information, or help making new connections. Those relationships I built made all the difference when challenging times occurred.

Dr. Nadine Kouba is a trained and certified professional executive coach. She works with leaders to increase their effectiveness and accelerate their business growth and profitability. Nadine brings a thoughtful approach to her coaching. She helps the client surface their goals and then create and work on an action plan that achieves their desired results—solving a business problem, handling a people issue, enhancing their communication, developing personal leadership, executive presence, or planning their career.

Dr. Kouba's professional credentials are a testament to her expertise. She is a Certified Professional Coach (PCC) through the International Coaching Federation (ICF), an international best-selling author, and a sought-after speaker.

Please scan the QR code to connect with this author.

Crystal Officer

Splendor

The winds didn't just blow, they howled, relentless and unforgiving, like waves crashing against a weathered shoreline, beating down on everything in their path. With each gust, it felt as though pieces of me were being stripped away, like leaves torn from a tree. I thought I was ready, strong enough to handle whatever life threw my way. But when the winds grew into storms, they pressed upon me testing my resilience and my faith.

The winds didn't come when I made the decision to move—they came when I arrived in a new region, away from everything familiar. I had left behind a life where I had thrived with friends who felt like family, a job I loved, and the comfort of having both of my daughters close by. Outwardly, everything seemed calm, but deep down, I knew something was missing. God was calling me somewhere new, and I trusted His voice, believing He had more for me.

My new chapter began with unexpected hurdles. On my very first day, I was rear-ended, my car totaled, and I was left questioning whether I was ready for the journey ahead. With one of my daughters and her cat, I found myself living in a Comfort Inn while the company I had just joined was in crisis. That's when grief found me. Not the kind of grief that comes with the loss of a loved one, but a subtle, shadowy kind that sneaks in without warning. It was the grief of leaving behind a season of life that I hadn't realized I was attached to. This wasn't an honest, clear grief; it lurked quietly in the corners of my mind, mourning the version of myself that was lost in transition. It was the silent farewell to a chapter of my life in which I thrived, that I had loved. I realized grief doesn't just visit us when we bury someone—it also arrives when we close a chapter of our lives that we loved.

As the winds of change swept through, grief settled in deeper, wrapping around my heart like a cold wind that whispered, *You've lost something you won't get back.* I couldn't help but look back. Turning toward what I had left behind, stuck in a past I could no longer live. Jesus tells us, *"Remember Lot's wife,"* and for the first time, I understood why. My heart was frozen in the "what was" while God was calling me into "what could be." But I couldn't alter my perspective, at least not yet. Then, the storms intensified.

One night, I found my daughter unconscious in a basement, surrounded by people who didn't care for her. My heart shattered. I half-carried her to the car, driving through the night, stopping repeatedly as she got sick. Each stop felt like a heavier burden—guilt, fear, failure—they all pressed down on me with the weight of a thousand storms. *I've failed her. I've failed as a mother.* It wasn't the first time, and I feared it wouldn't be the last.

Yet, as I drove through the night, something shifted within me. Thank you, Jesus. She's alive, and she's with me. What had begun as a night steeped in fear and guilt slowly transformed. It became a night filled with grace—grace I could see, feel, and finally understand. While loneliness and uncertainty weighed heavily on me, I felt God's presence break through, like sunlight cutting through heavy clouds. In that moment, He whispered to me, "This is the abundance of grace." His grace was not about stopping the storm but about carrying me through it. It was about giving me the strength to speak life into my daughter, offering her love and hope in her moment of need. I was not alone. Grace was there, wrapping around me. I clung to His extension of grace with everything I had, knowing His hand was not just on her life but on mine, guiding us both through the storm

But the storm didn't end there and the weight of everything continued to press down on me, heavier with each passing day. Working as a new CEO of a company in crisis was no small feat. I entered what I describe as my "I can't breathe" season, where everything felt critical, and internal conflicts were escalating. The winds of pressure and anxiety battered me from every side. Expectations were sky-high, and the responsibilities were heavy. But the people we served were special, deserving nothing short of excellence, and I knew I couldn't let them down. Despite the over-whelming challenges, I kept searching for reasons to stand. I couldn't afford to fail. Yet it wasn't just about me standing. We stood together, and as a team, we rose above the chaos. Together, we exceeded expectations, achieving things I never thought possible in such difficult circumstances.

I learned something profound in those moments. I learned how to compartmentalize my emotions under stress, to pace myself, and, most importantly, to survive. Gratitude became my lifeline. Each morning, I thanked God for the strength to rise, for the people fighting alongside me, and for every small victory, no matter how tiny. Every breath I took became an act of praise. It was faith that everything would work together for my good and believing that God is always faithful that carried me through.

The storms raged on, relentless, and soon the weight began to show. The physical toll was undeniable—as the responsibilities grew, so did the burden I carried. I gained 100 pounds, each pound a reflection of the emotional and spiritual weight I held onto. I was like a tree in the wind, catching leaves as they blew away, desperately trying to hold onto every-thing—the good and the bad. My body bore the brunt of that fight. The storms were heavy, but I never fell. I bent. I swayed. But I didn't break.

Resilience, I realized, wasn't about standing tall without bending or resisting life's winds. It's being deeply rooted, allowing myself to bend with the storms, understanding that there is strength in flexibility. It meant trusting that, even when I couldn't see the way forward, God's grace was sufficient. I had to release my need for certainty, let go of the burdens of fear and failure, and trust that God would carry me through the storm as He always had.

I came to understand that the resilience God was cultivating in me wasn't just for my benefit. As a leader, I learned that resilience is something you nurture within your team. I had to model vulnerability, demonstrating that it's okay to bend under pressure—but never to break. I encouraged my team to find their own roots, to ground themselves in their values, and to lean on one another when the winds grew strong. Together, we built a culture of trust, where vulnerability wasn't seen as weakness but as a path to growth. We focused on solutions, celebrating both small and big wins, even in the midst of chaos. I realized that leading through a storm isn't about having all the answers, it is standing firm in faith, adapting when needed, and empowering others to do the same.

But I would be remiss—doing a disservice—if I didn't acknowledge that during this season, under the weight of so many storms, the enemy crept in with his lies: "You're not strong enough. You're failing. Just give up. God doesn't love you." The darkness tried to close in on me, and in my most exhausted moments, the enemy whispered that ending it all was the only way out.

Yet, in those darkest moments, God's Word rose up in me, cutting through the lies like a sword: "God loves me. God is with me. God will never leave or forsake me. I am blessed. The glory of my latter house will be greater than the glory of my former house" (Haggai 2:9). I believed it. I clung to it. "The blood of the Lamb and the word of my testimony"— that's how I overcame (Revelation 12:11). His presence, His promises, and His witness in my life became my anchor in the storm.

I often reflect on the story of the Shunammite woman from 2 Kings 4, a narrative God has inscribed deeply on my heart. Like me, she faced a devastating storm—her son lay lifeless on a bed—but she didn't crumble under the weight of despair. Instead, with unwavering faith, she declared, "All shall be well." Her steadfast trust in God became a model for my own journey. She spoke life into her circumstances, refusing to let the storm define her. Even when everything seemed hopeless, she believed in God's power to restore.

To the women reading this: Storms will come. Life's winds will try to knock you down, but like a deeply rooted tree, your strength isn't in resisting the storm—it's in your roots. No matter how fierce the winds are, you will bend, but you will not break. As Isaiah 61:3 says, "They will be called oaks of righteousness, a planting of the Lord for the display of His splendor."

As I navigated the storms of my life and leadership, I found that silence often spoke louder than words. In the midst of chaos, I learned to lean into the stillness, where God's guidance became clearest. Those quiet moments revealed a deeper truth: great leadership isn't just about decisive action—it's about clarity in chaos, emotional resilience, and the discernment to listen for the quiet whispers of wisdom. In stillness, I found strength and renewal, allowing me to lead with greater wisdom and purpose.

A select passage from "Soul Journer," a series of poems by Crystal Officer

The significance of silence,
Light shines through the dark,
An anointings being carried,
Speaking life into deep parts.

Three wells in the valley,
Under heavy dispute,
Famine in the desert,
His grace carries you.

Unseen realities,
A rain cloud pursues,
Sparrows in the morning,
Divine food nourishes you.

The substance of things hoped for,
The evidence of things unseen,
Strength perfected in weakness,
His glory to be seen.

Wisdom builds a house,
Knowledge applies to hearts,
Living water to be found,
In the place where love abounds.

Crystal Officer is a visionary executive leader and dynamic change agent dedicated to driving transformative initiatives within the nonprofit sector. She holds a Master's in Public Administration from Murray State University and is currently pursuing a Doctor of Philosophy in General Psychology with a focus on Industrial and Organizational Psychology, further equipping her to enhance organizational effectiveness. Crystal also has a Certificate in Corporate Communication from Cornell University, a Certificate of Specialization in Strategy from Harvard Business School Online, and is certified in EQ-i 2.0 and EQ 360.

Passionate about fostering positive work environments, Crystal implements strategies that empower individuals and promote collaboration. Her powerful insights inspire audiences to confront challenges head-on while cultivating atmospheres that drive operational excellence. In her personal time, she enjoys playing the cello and cherishes moments with her two daughters, Hope and Faith.

Please scan the QR code to connect with this author.

Shannon Shores

Dear Younger Me:
Lessons from Fierce Women

Dear Little Shannon,

This chapter is dedicated to you. Remember reading the book *The Monster at the End of this Book* with Grover? Even though you knew the ending, you would get anxious with every turn of the page. With each turning page, you thought the ending may change from him being relieved that the monster was just cuddly ole him to being a real monster. Lil Shannon, I am here to tell you that you will experience real-life "monsters" throughout your life, but the ending will be the same as Grover. You win!

Let's focus on your winning strategy, Shannon. You will learn what love is and is not. You will learn that love should not come with a price or consequence. You will learn to be the hero and not the victim in your story. You will learn these life-changing lessons by paying attention to some of the most amazing and fierce women in your life.

Nobody Picks on "SZ"

Grade school was not an easy place for you. You never felt like you fit in because you were insecure about your clothes, glasses, and big ears. You will get picked on and cower down from bullies. One day, you witness a bully picking on a student in the hallway. You witness SZ pick up a cafeteria tray and smack the bully over the head to get him to stop. You are not big on violence, but you want so much to have that much confidence to stand up to others. SZ was your hero that day and for the others he was picking on.

You will grow up to realize that bullies do not go away, but you will find your SZ internal power. Surprisingly, you will grow up, and people will think your personality is too much. They will say you can be pushy, opinionated, and just "too much" at times. Guess what? You grew into the person you were always meant to be. A leader that believes the good in people and works to help them find the best in themselves. An entrepreneur who loves to take mismatched pieces and build beautiful things in life and business. A kindhearted badass who gives a voice to people who are scared or unable to use theirs. People may say you are too much, and you will say, "Go find less!"

Fake It till You Make It

You will make it to the state-level speech competition with a speech on recycling. I can still remember how the teacher told you how to use hand gestures when you said "reuse, reduce, and recycle." Maybe this is where your speaking with hand gestures began. Either way, you did find that you loved public speaking. Even though you were afraid to use your voice for other things, public speaking gave you a way to organize your thoughts in a structured way to get your point across.

When you get to high school, your speech teacher will leave you a lasting message, "Fake it till you make it." This phrase was to remind you that the audience doesn't know how you are feeling or thinking unless you tell them. You will use this phrase as a reminder for when you are speaking and forget what you were saying midsentence during a presentation. Just keep going! You will use this when you are in a conflict or difficult conversation. You will want to shrink like you did all those years ago in the hallway, but instead, you step on your foot to drive your attention there instead of crying. Just keep going! "Fake it till you make it" is a battle cry for all of us not to second-guess ourselves or be critical, but to know who you are and keep going.

Never Say "No" to an Opportunity

When you take your first job out of graduate school, you will get an opportunity to work with a woman full of spunk and strength. You will be amazed at how she walks into a room and the confidence she brings with her with every step. She is a social worker just like you, but she is the CEO of the company. Yep, a social worker leading a company, and you wanted to learn everything about her.

One day, you approach her and ask how she became the leader she was. She will tell you something that you will use in your career that will help you break through ceilings. The ingredient of her success was "never say no to any opportunity." This means learning from others no matter what it is. Do you want to learn budgets? Yes! Would you like to present on a topic? Absolutely! This no-nonsense thinking will propel your career because you take every opportunity that comes to you. Some opportunities were tougher than some, but you learned from some of the best, and you learned things you would have never achieved on your own.

Do You Want to Be the Cat or the Mouse?

Because of opportunities that came to you, you will take a big jump in life and become CEO of a company. A small-town girl takes her social work degree and runs a successful company. Success was not easy. You will attend a business seminar about growing your business. On the stage, you will see this beautiful woman with blonde hair without a strand of hair out of place. She spoke with such elegance, and you thought if you could only have an ounce of what she had that you would be on the right track.

After the meeting, you get the chance to meet her, and you decide to work together. She helped you for a couple of years to build and grow your business. How did you do it? During one of those meetings, you were struggling with a business issue and she asked, "Do you want to be the mouse or the cat?" In this situation, you were being the mouse. You were being weak. You were settling for less than you deserved. You were allowing others to dictate your actions. You decide in that moment that you would always strive to be the cat.

Time for a J. Crew Sale

Love and friendship won't always be easy. You'll face heartache, betrayal, and moments of disappointment. But along the way, you'll also find true love and genuine friendship—the kind that fills your soul. Some friends will be your loudest cheerleaders, while others will teach you they don't belong in your tribe.

In your tribe, a "J. Crew Sale" becomes the secret rallying cry. It's code for "Someone needs support." When the call goes out, no one hesitates. The tribe gathers, lifting each other up; no judgment, just love. Your crew may be small, but they are fierce, loyal, and always have your back—no matter what life throws at you.

Don't Be a B!#ch, He's Cute

You probably think that boys are overrated and not worth the hassle. Puberty was not the easiest thing. In seventh grade, AP is going to tell everyone at school you have a p*nis because you won't do some of the other things girls are doing with boys. As humiliating as that was, you will grow older to discover that love can be a rollercoaster. Sometimes, love isn't what you think it is, but you will be proud when love figures it out. Love will also mask things like addiction that will bring sadness, loss, and pain in your life. Even though love won't be easy, you will still search for the love like you dreamed of between Brenda and Dylan in 90210.

Searching won't be easy. You will close yourself off because you will be convinced that your picker is broken. It will take a perfect "wing woman" to push you into the arms of someone during a time when both of your lives are chaotic and not ideal for love. You will discover someone who loves you for you—the good, the bad, the nerdy. He will be part of your story of helping you find your spirit, unapologetic attitude, and the desire to always want more. You will learn that love isn't perfect, but it is caring, nurturing, and always supportive of all your big ideas. You will learn that true love stories truly do not have endings.

Get Up, Show Up, Dress Up

Grandma "O" was the ultimate fashionista. She always reminded you that looking fabulous was essential—especially if you scored it on sale! As she neared her 90th birthday, you made sure she had everything she requested, even though she wasn't feeling well enough to fully enjoy it. Still, the cake, cherry pie, tiny Coca-Colas, and a sparkling tiara were all there, fit for the birthday queen. Just weeks later, she passed away, but her greatest lesson stuck with you forever.

Being a fashionista on a budget, she taught you that how you show up speaks volumes about how you feel. Dressing up and looking sharp became your armor. On days when life felt too heavy to even get out of bed—when you wanted to skip that big presentation or avoid solving someone else's problem—her words echoed in your mind: show up and make an impact. As a kid, you were often overlooked, rarely using your voice. But as an adult? Your presence, smile, and killer outfit make sure people know you're in the room.

You Will Know When You Get There

After a big loss, you found yourself trapped in a loop—work, sleep, repeat. Months passed before you finally realized, "I need help." So, you made an appointment with a therapist, poured your heart out about the loss and your lingering depression, and then asked, "How will I know when I find happiness?" Her response? A vague, "You'll know when you get there."

At first, you will think, "Really? I'm paying for this?" But in time, her words start to click. She was absolutely right. You spend the next 15+ years chasing happiness, only to discover you had the power all along. Happiness wasn't something to find, buy, or stumble into—it was inside you all along.

Happiness became the fuel that got you out of bed, drove you to want more from life, and allowed you to surround yourself with good vibes and distance from the toxic ones. Happiness is saying "yes" to things that make your heart leap and "no" to the things that don't, guilt-free. It's the realization that you've had the key to your own joy the entire time.

You made it to the end, and just like with Grover, you win! Thank you for loving me and pushing for more. Your win comes with a beautiful family, amazing friends, and countless life lessons that you will continue to learn. You will grow the most during the most uncomfortable times of your life, but because of the lessons you have learned and the tribe around you, you will keep moving.

What is next for you? It would be selfish not to continue to share these life lessons with other women who desire more. As a tribute to your beautiful grandmothers and their lessons of strength and tenacity, Bertie Mae Consulting has been born. Through this tribute, you will help other women find their "more" and remove the barriers that get in their way of their defined success. This effort is fueled by your grandmas but also the countless number of fierce women who helped you along the way. *Always remember to turn around and lift up the next person—because empowered women empower women.* This is just the beginning of something magical.

Best,
Shannon

Shannon Shores is a force of nature fueled by energy, creativity, and an unstoppable drive to empower women. With her background in social work, Shannon expertly navigates personalities and values differences, using those strengths to build thriving businesses and dynamic teams. She's a master builder, transforming diverse elements into something extraordinary. Now, through Bertie Mae Consulting, Shannon is on a mission to help women unleash their inner greatness, breaking barriers and tapping into their "beast mode" to conquer every challenge. She's here to inspire, uplift, and ignite your potential!

Please scan the QR code to connect with this author.

Lisa Loyet Schmitz

Too Young to Be Beige

The year was 1997. My 30th birthday had been celebrated gloriously! Life seemed good—two toddler boys kept life full of fun and joy, my freelance graphic design business was thriving, I volunteered for some great causes, we were in family playgroups, and I was blessed with an abundance of family and friends. I was mastering the art of juggling it all and being everything to everyone.

But was I? After reviewing photos taken during a birthday trip, it struck me. I was beige. As this person in the photo looked at me, I wondered who she was. This person was beige from head to foot. Hair, skin, shirt, pants, shoes, and expression. What the hell? This wasn't me! The problem was, I honestly didn't know who I was, but I was certainly too young to be beige!

When first asked to be part of *Living Well with GRIT* by telling my story, I wondered why. What do I have to offer that others haven't already said? After all, we have all dealt with things—personal and professional. What could I say that would inspire and encourage others to overcome obstacles and grow and flourish in their own lives? Then I decided that maybe I don't need to say anything new but to remind women that at any age, we don't need to be everything to everyone because, in those attempts, we sometimes push ourselves to erasure, to the point of becoming beige.

Most women juggle a lot in our daily lives and, like me, thrive on it. I positively love having a full calendar that includes family, friends, and work. What I was starting to realize is that personal time was needed to balance the scales. I set forth with a new goal: finding what wasn't working and trying to change it.

The first thing I wanted to change was to not be beige! I had always been one of those girls who would wear the latest fashions, color, or cut my hair drastically on a whim, and push the boundaries with mixing and matching hats, jewelry, jackets, and shoes. Shoes. It somehow always goes back to shoes. Looking back, it's all kind of funny, but at the time, it was liberating—it was "Breaking Beige!"

First, my hair. I went to the drugstore, bought a box of "Cherry Cola" dye, and went home to begin the metamorphosis. Now, with some momentum, I took the initiative to ask my then husband if we could meet friends and go out for an adult evening. He agreed, and I hit my closet, looking for anything except beige. It was then that a box in my closet appeared to glow with a "pick me" aura. This was a very special box, but I had not yet realized its power.

About six months prior, my mother-in-law treated me to an afternoon of lunch and shopping. I had mentioned the dread of becoming a frumpy mom who didn't take time for herself. She told me that I had complete control of this and it was important to not lose my spunk or my individuality. To allow myself to feel fun, frisky, and fabulous! When we returned from that shopping trip, she took me to her closet and brought down a white box labeled "Black Suede Dress Boots."

She lovingly opened the box and revealed the most stunning high-heeled knee boots I had ever seen. With a nostalgic look in her eyes, she proceeded to tell me that after she had children, she decided she was not going to become a frumpy mom, donning only sweatpants and slippers. She then shared with me that at times when she needed to remind herself that she was more than a wife and mother, she would get dressed up, put on these boots, and go out. She may have referred to them as "magic" (if not, I bestowed that quality to them). She handed those magic boots to me, passing them on, saying, "You now have these ready when needed."

They were needed in December 1997. With my new hair color and magic boots, I had the top and bottom of my "I'm a badass" outfit well on its way! I opted for a black double-breasted blazer, black shorts, and fishnets. I'm pretty certain no one recognized me that night.

But it wasn't so much what happened to me on the outside—that paled in comparison to what was happening on the inside. I was tired of giving so much only to be told it wasn't enough and I wasn't good enough. I *was,* and I was about to start proving it. Where did that start? It had only one place to start—with *me*! I needed to believe in myself again, to stop trying to be everything to everyone, and find balance in what was the most important in my life—my family, my job, and myself.

For a while, it seemed to be working. I trained for a marathon and subsequently ran four of them. I focused more on being present with my kids rather than just being there. Some of my friendships flourished, while others took the natural process of fading away. Life seemed good again. But was it?

During this time, the one thing that I was trying to avoid thinking about was that my then husband and I did not seem to be on the same page. Things had changed. Had he changed? I don't think so. Had I? Yes. But this isn't a divorce drama story. We just grew apart, and I'll leave it at that. I was challenged with a family life where we were merely existing in the same household. Was this the example I wanted for my children? It wasn't. Don't get me wrong, divorce is never easy. But rather than drag it out for years, saying we were staying together "for the kids" was not the choice that was made, and we divorced.

Through all this, I never questioned my career choice. Believing that being an art director and graphic designer was my calling, I was determined to do everything I could to keep that fire ablaze, even if it meant taking a second job on the nights when I didn't have my boys.

What I discovered during this time was that I wish I could have told my younger self to not stew over:

1) Being an entrepreneur doesn't mean you are not a professional. Being self-employed is a real job—don't let anyone ever try to tell you otherwise, and 2) The corporate world is full of egotistical people that you have every right to stand up to. And it is also full of wonderful people who want you to succeed.

Early on, I encountered a boss who, at the time, I thought was a real jerk. He was tough. I didn't think he liked me, and I couldn't wait to move out of his department—which eventually happened. It was during that time I realized he had given me some great advice and truly was an advocate for my success. Years later, I wrote him a thank-you note, which he acknowledged during his retirement party, which I was invited to many years (and jobs) later.

The words of advice he gave me are those I have shared with my children, countless groups of students during career fairs and presentations, and interns who have worked for me over the years. In no particular order, these gems are:

- Don't burn bridges. You never know when you will come across someone again. That person who is an intern today could be running a department or a company you want to be part of in the future.

- Don't dress for the job you have; dress for the job you want. Get up every day, even the days you work from home, and prepare yourself from head to toe in the manner you would when meeting with the most important person you know.

- Find a mentor and let them know you aspire to be like them—ask questions, follow their lead. You can learn a lot from observing, and you never know who that mentor might introduce you to.

- Take notes. Your greatest tool is to be informed. Ask questions. Write it all down. Communication is key.

Fast forward to the present. My husband, Craig, and I have been married for seventeen years. We met via mutual friends—neither one of us looking for someone, nor were we set up on a date. It just happened. We took our time introducing our children—my two and his three, and they became our five. The kids were all pretty close in age, and we had already established that if they didn't get along, our relationship would not progress beyond friendship. They did, and we have been fortunate, but we have also worked hard to be a blended family. Raising five children was packed with excitement, fun, challenges, and lots of activities!

During this time, I was fortunate that my self-employment allowed the flexibility to be actively involved in each of their lives—be it school, doctor/dentist/ortho appointments, field trips, Girl Scouts, hockey, baseball, soccer, volleyball, swimming, football, rugby, parent/teacher conferences, art exhibits, learning how to drive, and applying to colleges. I was able to manage my schedule to fit it all in. When our youngest was almost 16, I was offered a full-time position with one of my footwear manufacturing clients and determined that I was ready to be back in an office, working as part of a team. To this day, I am fortunate to have continued my passion to work as a marketing/creative director in the shoe industry.

Reflecting on all the events that shaped who I have become up to this point and who I want to be going forward, there are three things that are the constant driving force. Belief. Hope. Faith.

When I was in my thirties, I **believed** I could be a better version of myself. It took a lot of courage and a lot of contemplation to reach that belief. I always believed I was capable of doing many things, but to be the best I could be, I needed to put myself first. This didn't mean I didn't love my family, my job, or my friends—it meant that I loved all of them so much that I knew I could do better for them.

After my divorce, I **hoped** that I had the strength and courage to take the necessary steps to protect myself and my children while we all adjusted to a different schedule and family arrangement. Having the optimism that everything would work out, even on the days where it felt impossible, helped me persevere and maintain belief that I could rise and achieve great things.

Through it all, it is **faith** that weaves it all together. The faith that if I believed in and allowed myself to hope for good things, that faith and spirituality would guide me in the right direction. This was summed up in the words of one of my favorite musicians, Dave Grohl, in his autobiography, *The Storyteller*: "Faith, the unconditional belief in something that defies logic and guides your life."

Looking back, I'm grateful for every opportunity but also every obstacle it took to bring the color back into my life. I realize now that every day we have a choice to put our best effort into something. Some days it will be our kids, others our partners. Oftentimes it will be our jobs or our volunteer outreach. Not every day will we be able to put ourselves first—but in order to be the best we can we need to try.

It all comes back to shoes. During a meeting with Renee Moore of *Kirkwood City Lifestyle* magazine, I noticed the cover of the January 2023 issue. It was a pair of boots that were on the cover of *G.R.I.T Resilience*. I commented on it, and Renee was shocked to learn I did not know Jennifer Bardot. She made the introduction, and Jennifer and I connected and hit it off immediately—both professionally and personally. Since that time, we have had countless opportunities to share our love of networking, meeting new people, and embracing new experiences. When Jennifer shared with me that shoes from my company, Ros Hommerson, were going to grace the cover and invited me to be an author, I was elated. This proves that we never stop learning, growing, and allowing ourselves the opportunity to let our colors shine!

With magic boots. Belief. Hope. Faith. And Grit.

Lisa is the Director of Marketing and Creative Development for the Drew Shoe Corp. Most of her career, she has been involved in the shoe industry in everything from modeling to marketing. Lisa holds a BA in Fashion Marketing and Fine Arts, plus an MA in Visual Communications, both from Lindenwood University, as well as a MicroMasters Certification in Digital Marketing from Curtin University.

During a 25-year entrepreneurial adventure, Lisa worked as an Art Director for many industries, including non-profit, agriculture, fashion, legal, food service, and entertainment. She was the Art Director for the Emmy-nominated Broadway show, "John Leguizamo's Sexaholix."

Lisa and her husband, Craig, love spending time with their five grown children and being part of their developing families, which now includes two beautiful grandchildren. She enjoys cooking, traveling, gardening, yoga, and going on long walks with Craig and their dog, Hope.

Please scan the QR code to connect with this author.

Dianna M. Paterline

Lessons in Resilience

When I was asked to write this chapter, I considered what I could possibly share that would be helpful for others. What struck me was much as doctors make the worst patients, coaches make the worst clients. I have spent my career helping leaders tap into their skills and recognize productive and non-productive behaviors. My goal is to help them love what they do and find their own success. Looking back over the last five years of my journey, I realized that I was not aware of the behaviors that were not supporting my success until I had no choice but to see.

I'm hoping that by sharing my personal journey through a cancer diagnosis and treatment, I can highlight the valuable lessons in resilience I've learned along the way. As a professional coach who suddenly found herself in the client's seat, I hope my experiences and insights will provide both inspiration and practical advice for leaders facing their own challenges.

2019 started as one of the best years of my life. I am married and have two adult children. In 2019, the oldest of my sons graduated from college and had strong prospects for landing his first job. My youngest son finished his first year in college and was doing well. My husband and I just celebrated our 25th wedding anniversary and were planning our dream, delayed honeymoon trip to Italy in June. At work, I was promoted from a senior-level individual contributor role to managing a team of 15. The new job started when I returned from Italy.

About a week before we left on our trip, I noticed a lump in my breast. I wasn't too concerned. I am susceptible to sebaceous cysts and assumed that was all it was. I had my annual mammography appointment scheduled right after we returned from our trip.

Italy was amazing, and I started my new job full of energy and excitement at the prospect of leading a team that had been without a manager for about four months. I met with the team and assured them I would be present to help and support them in their continued growth and success.

At my mammography appointment, I found out I was correct. The lump I felt was just a benign cyst. However, because I raised a concern, they had taken a closer look, and they did find a lump further up in my breast that was later confirmed to be cancer.

Suddenly, the world seemed to come to a screeching halt.

My family did not have a history of cancer, and the news took me and my husband by surprise. There were a lot of tears initially as I adjusted to my new reality—I had cancer. The news felt overwhelming. Fortunately, I have access to one of the best cancer groups in the United States through Washington University and the Siteman Cancer Center. A team of doctors was quickly assembled, and I started on my new journey. There was some good news. We had caught the cancer early, and my team was optimistic about my chances for a full recovery. On the not-so-encouraging side, my score from my Oncotype DX test (a tumor profiling test) had come back with a higher than desired score. A good score was 10 or less. I had a 27. This landed me in the high-risk category for the cancer to return. It also cemented my treatment plan to include chemotherapy, radiation, and hormone therapy.

I have always been a naturally resilient and confident person. Those strengths kicked in and helped at first. My husband and I met with the surgeon and the oncologist and made a plan. I always function better when I have a plan. I also made the decision to continue to work during chemotherapy and radiation. I told myself it was for the benefit of my team. They had waited so long for a leader; I didn't want to leave them in a lurch until I finished my treatment. By making these decisions, I convinced myself I was still in charge.

The lumpectomy surgery was successful, and I launched into my four months of chemotherapy. For anyone who has never experienced chemo, let me just say, it is not for sissies. Chemotherapy is an incredibly challenging experience, both physically and mentally. It tests one's endurance and resilience in ways that are difficult to imagine. The best analogy I can use is it's like being on a continuous roller coaster that you can't exit. The chemotherapy process was cyclical—periods of relative wellness followed by days of extreme difficulty. This pattern repeated eight times over four months, testing my endurance and resolve each time.

One of the first and starkest lessons I learned about behaviors that did not support me was that I was terrible at asking for help. Have you ever found yourself in a situation where your usual strengths seemed inadequate?

As I navigated my cancer journey, I discovered that even as a coach, I had much to learn about asking for help and allowing others to support me. I suddenly needed friends to help drive me to and from my chemo appointments, my hairdresser met me after hours to shave my head, and my husband and oldest son had to care for almost every need during the bottom of my roller coaster rides. At work, my administrative assistant became the guardian of my calendar. During treatment weeks, she refused to allow any meetings starting Thursday afternoon and all day Friday as I plunged into my chemo bottoms. It was incredibly hard for me to admit that I could not do it all myself.

My experience highlights a common challenge many leaders face: the struggle to balance self-reliance with the ability to accept support. Recognizing when to lean on others is a crucial skill in both personal crises and professional leadership.

To ease my discomfort at asking for help, I kept the support group small. I only let in those that had to know. Again, I told myself I didn't want to make a social media splash out of my illness. I am a private person, and no one who was not directly involved needed to know. This included not telling a couple of my best and closest friends. They did not live close, so I didn't need to tell them. I did meet up with my friend and roommate from college over Christmas. When we met, she was understandably shocked when she saw my bald head and learned about the cancer. What I did not count on was how hurt she was that I did not tell her earlier.

While my team at work was aware, I was careful not to make my illness the center of discussions. I wanted the team to focus on work, not on me. Despite my efforts, they were kind and continued to check up on me and my progress. I even refused to let my sister come stay with me. I told myself there was nothing for her to do other than watch me sleep on the couch.

Just as I thought I was regaining control of my life post-treatment, another unexpected challenge arose, further testing my resilience and reinforcing the lessons I was learning about impact and accepting help. Fast forward to spring of 2020. I finished my four months of chemo and four months of radiation. The pandemic had become real, and my family had been locked down in our house for a couple of months. At the end of May, I was feeling much better and decided the family should go for a hike in a beautiful state park near us. About three miles into our six-mile hike, I took the wrong step and broke my ankle. I spent two hours propped up on my son's back in the middle of a poison ivy patch, waiting to be picked up. Two days later, I now have a metal plate and thirteen screws in my ankle as well as a raging allergic reaction to the poison ivy on my arm.

Once again, I found myself helpless and completely dependent on those around me. I worked the next two months from the recliner as I hopped and crawled around my house. At this point, my sister chose to ignore my insistence that I did not need help and drove four hours both ways in a day to celebrate my birthday. It was amazing how good her visit made me feel.

The next realization about non-supportive behaviors came slower than the first, but it did come. I realized that while my journey was a personal one, my life and events that happened to me did not occur in a vacuum. My unwillingness to let others in during my journey not only hurt me but also hurt those around me. I was not benefiting from the love, care, and support my friends and family could provide, and they were not getting the opportunity to show me the friendship and provide the help they deeply wanted to.

As I apply these lessons in my coaching, I emphasize with leaders that it is important to recognize that our behaviors and actions have reach and that none of us exist in a bubble. Be cautious not to assume too narrow of a perspective.

I am four years into my cancer journey and am very happy to say I continue to be healthy and cancer-free. As I celebrated this milestone, I also reflected on how my experiences have hopefully made me a wiser, more thoughtful, and compassionate wife, mother, friend, leader, coach, and person. Circling back to where we started, the coach in me would like to share what I have learned in hopes that it helps others in their development journeys.

Here are the five lessons in resilient behaviors I have learned. As you read through these lessons, I encourage you to reflect on your own experiences. How might these insights apply to challenges you're facing, whether in your personal life or your leadership role?

1. **Tenacity**: Regardless of the circumstances, it is important never to give up. My surgeon told me on multiple occasions that my positive outlook and sense of humor would help contribute to a successful outcome.

2. **Vision**: Having a clear sense of purpose and direction is essential to achieving anything. My vision was and continues to be to live a long and healthy life by listening to my doctors and taking care of myself.

3. **Collaboration**: Never underestimate the importance of a strong network. Whether you are trying to accomplish a task at work, find a new job, or deal with a personal crisis, the people in your network are crucial for your success. Recognize when you need help, and don't be afraid to ask.

4. **The Power of Connection**: Life does not occur in a vacuum. Everything we do impacts us and those around us. One of my favorite leadership quotes comes from Kip Tindell, chairman and chief executive officer of The Container Store: "Everything you do and everything you don't do affects the people around you and your business, far, far more than you realize." We all create our own wake and should never ignore how our wake affects those around us.

5. **Well-being**: It is easy to let stressors and problems take over our lives at the expense of our health. Had I not prioritized my annual health exams, I may not be here today to write this chapter. Nothing is more important than your own health. Take good care and prioritize yourself.

As leaders, we often focus on guiding others through challenges. But my journey has reinforced that our own growth and resilience are equally important. I encourage you to regularly assess your own behaviors, seek support when needed, and prioritize your well-being. By doing so, you'll not only navigate your personal challenges more effectively but also become a more empathetic and resilient leader.

Dianna M. Paterline is a seasoned talent leader based in St. Louis, MO. With a career spanning over two decades in financial services, Dianna has established herself as a strategic partner in succession planning, leadership development, and organizational effectiveness. Her expertise includes performance management, executive coaching, and fostering high-performing teams.

Dianna holds a BS in Business Administration from the University of Kansas and numerous professional certifications, including the International Coaching Federation (ICF) Accredited Certified Coach (ACC) and Hudson Institute Certified Coach.

When not working, Dianna loves to spend time with her husband and two sons. On the weekend, you will often find her and her husband rummaging in dusty antique stores, looking for treasured pieces of history.

Please scan the QR code to connect with this author.

Danielle Singer

Finding the Joy in Being Enough

I grew up in the '80s and '90s as the proud child of a family with a black cherry minivan (complete with wood paneling), a bag phone in our car, and by my teenage years, dialup internet and AOL on our home computer. Like so many children of that era, I also had instilled in me the belief that women could—and should—have it all: a family, an education, a career, hobbies, the ability to travel, and free time to boot.

I started stacking up wins, graduating early and with honors, landing my first job before graduation, getting married, buying a house, and planning to start a family. Initially, everything went according to plan, and within a few years, I was promoted to my first leadership role and began pursuing my master's degree. However, I soon discovered that marriage required more nurturing than I had anticipated, home ownership came with expenses that chip away at the travel budget, and starting a family proved more challenging than I had hoped.

To top it off, my first experience in leadership was humbling, making me question my abilities and whether I was in the right seat—or even on the right career bus. After years of heartache trying to start a family, I faced the devastating loss of my first pregnancy and found the path to becoming a foster or adoptive parent to be daunting, too. Life seemed to be throwing insurmountable obstacles at every turn. My carefully curated future of "having it all" was crumbling before it had even started, and I felt lost in a life that looked so different from what I had imagined.

After a mentor encouraged me to leverage my strengths and shift my mindset, I began to reflect on my struggles. I was progressing toward my goal, so why did I feel overwhelmed? Before I could make meaningful progress, my "overwhelm" started to unwind, and I chalked it up to a temporary run of bad luck. In the coming years, my husband and I were blessed with the family we had hoped for, I continued to grow my career while he grew his business, I pursued hobbies, we traveled, and I learned to navigate the chaos. Things were back on track.

When I tell you I was breezing into the year 2020, feeling like I was thriving, you can imagine the punchline I didn't see coming. By this time, I had a growing family, a growing career, and I was progressing through an MBA program when the pandemic struck. My husband's business faced significant challenges while I juggled remote work, a remote elementary schooler, and losing daycare for my two children under age 2. I started waking up at 3 a.m. to work before taking over childcare at midday, all while facing new personal health challenges. Once again, the obstacles felt insurmountable.

In 2021, I found myself again in a better place. I earned a promotion in late 2020 and was feeling proficient in my new role and in virtual work. Daycare and schools had reopened, and a new normalcy took hold. I realized I needed a mindset shift...and to build my grit. Through this reflection came several hard realizations: I was letting life happen *to* me and had been so misguided to think I could achieve all the glory without also enduring any of the struggles. That's when I came to the realization that the childhood credo of having it all was overwhelming. What if, instead, I focused on having *enough*?

In embracing this new mindset, I also accepted the idea that "enough" did not equate to failure. I let go of the story I had been telling myself, which was if I had the capacity to do more and chose not to, I was not living up to my true potential. Shifting my perspective also allowed me to see the cyclical nature of setbacks and successes. Rather than trying to focus on how to "fix myself," this time I focused on taking control and owning my grit. Instead of waiting out the hard times, I needed to move forward with intention, and I discovered a few key principles that helped me take control, celebrate my successes, and find the joy in being enough.

It comes down to this:

1. **Comparison is the Thief of Joy:** I started comparing my results to where I was a year ago and not to the highlight reels of others. There will always be someone else with more, and while it may appear they've had more successes, undoubtedly, they've encountered more failures, too.

2. **"No" Is a Complete Sentence:** Using the sentence "No." doesn't require justification or explanation. Saying no is really just saying yes to being fully invested in current commitments. Success is so often found in what we choose *not* to do.

3. **Ask for Help:** Rebuilding my network post-pandemic was daunting, but setting small goals and seeking advice led to renewed connections and support.

4. **Personal Purpose:** Prioritizing where and how I spend my time and energy has made all the difference. By aligning my values, beliefs, and goals with my career, community involvement, and hobbies, I've discovered greater meaning in fewer commitments. This has shown me the beauty of being intentional and striving for enough versus trying to do and have it all.

5. **Cultivate My Grit:** Finding my grit has allowed me to see that challenges are actually just stepping stones and reminded me that I have the tools to overcome obstacles if I simply trust myself.

As I reflect on my journey, I recognize that while it hasn't unfolded like I expected, it has led to a richer and more fulfilling life than I could have imagined. Making time for reflection has shown me that every setback has yielded a valuable lesson. In the pursuit of a purposeful life, progress matters more than perfection, and having grit is essential along the way. Besides, how many of us are happier serving as neighborhood trustees? Sometimes, saying no really can be more fulfilling.

Danielle Singer is a seasoned veteran in the financial services industry, bringing 20 years of experience in service delivery and technology. As the Director of Service Enablement, she spearheads strategic initiatives that enhance the customer service experience. Her responsibilities encompass business planning, business agility, change management, communication, and transformation leadership capabilities that accelerate value delivery to clients, colleagues, and the community.

Additionally, Danielle is passionate about leadership development and fostering an inclusive workplace culture. Through her role as leader of the Edward Jones Women's Leadership Collaborative, Danielle plays a pivotal role in cultivating networks and development among women leaders at her firm. She contributes to multiple enterprise Diversity, Equity, and Inclusion initiatives, serves as a community leader on municipality committees, and as Chairperson for the Women's Leadership Network at Beyond Housing.

Please scan the QR code to connect with this author.

Eli Knight

Crafting Connections through GRIT

Looking back on my childhood, it's clear that the groundwork for who I am today was laid in the midst of chaos. Growing up in a blended family with my mom and four siblings, I witnessed the impact of trauma first-hand. My mom, the youngest of nine children raised in poverty, endured her own struggles early in life, which manifested in ways I couldn't fully understand at the time. Diagnosed with bipolar and schizophrenia in her early twenties, her life spiraled downward due to a series of bad decisions and substance abuse, unraveling both her world and ours. At some point, the weight of raising us became too much, and my siblings and I were separated to go on and live with our respective fathers. It was a confusing time; I couldn't comprehend why she could no longer care for us.

As the second oldest and the more outgoing sibling, I became the "strong one," stepping into a matriarchal role at a young age. People often told me I was just like my mother, and while I loved her, I knew deep down that I didn't want that to be my path. I didn't want to carry her trauma into my adulthood. Having a mother addicted to drugs and ultimately choosing that life over getting clean and raising her children would be defining to my own sense of self-worth and belonging. If my own mother didn't want to care for us anymore, then how could I also continue to rely on people as I grew up?

I realize how incredibly fortunate I am to have had a tremendous father who stepped in when my mother couldn't. In a way, what I lost with my mother, I gained tenfold with my father, who provided the stability, guidance, and love that I needed to navigate my formative years. And it's ironic—though bittersweet—that my siblings and I were blessed with fathers who connected with each other, ensuring that despite the chaos in our mother's life, we remained close as a family. Our fathers worked together to make sure that we, as siblings, grew up with a strong bond, and I can attribute much of my close relationship with them to the support they provided. Additionally, I've been incredibly lucky to have an amazing "bonus" mom—my stepmother—who was there for me through it all. She stepped up to the plate and, alongside my father, created an environment of love, strength, and resilience that helped shape the person I am today. I can confidently say that my success today is a direct result of their unwavering support and the powerful connections they nurtured in our family.

I unknowingly set myself up with the belief that I must do everything I can to avoid falling into the same spiral of despair and heartbreak my mother created at all costs. I convinced myself that success meant ticking off all the conventional boxes—graduating college, starting a career, building a family, and achieving the life society defines as "successful." But as I began that journey, I quickly realized I didn't have a clear vision of what that life actually looked like for me. I enrolled in college, taking courses in subjects I had always excelled at, thinking it would somehow lead to a fulfilling path. Yet, something was missing. I found myself accumulating a mountain of debt without any real sense of direction, and it hit me that I was moving forward blindly. I had to make the difficult decision to drop out and essentially "start over," which felt, at the time, like a massive failure. I wasn't sure what to do next, but I kept moving.

During that period, while taking general education courses at the community college, I started a job at a new restaurant, and just days into training, I was offered a management position. What I didn't realize at the time was that they were seeing something in me—those soft skills I had developed growing up as the "strong one" for my siblings, leading them through our chaotic upbringing.

Managing people and processes came naturally, and I had an "aha" moment: I could turn these skills into a career. That was when I started to think about the construction industry, the field my father had always been a part of and had encouraged me to pursue since high school. At the time, I dismissed his advice, thinking I needed to carve my own path. But little did I know, he could see the potential in me that I had been too blind to recognize in myself. It took stepping away from what I thought my path was supposed to look like to realize my own capabilities.

When I started my career path, it was my father's connections that got my foot in the door in the construction industry. That sense of connection—both within my family and in my career—has been a central force in my journey. And as I navigated this male-dominated field, I leaned on those relationships to learn, grow, and find my place. Over a decade later, I can trace every point of success back to the relationships I've built along the way. It's a testament to the power of connection: while grit kept me moving forward, it was the people in my life who supported, mentored, and lifted me when I needed it most.

Of all the qualities encompassed by grit, tenacity is perhaps the one that has carried me through the most difficult moments. But as I reflect, I realize that even my tenacity was often fueled by the people I connected with along the way. When I think back on my journey, my sheer willpower certainly kept me moving through the setbacks—the moments when it felt easier to quit than to push forward. Yet, it was also the encouragement of others that reminded me I didn't have to walk the path alone. Tenacity might have kept me standing, but it was the support from the relationships I had fostered that helped me rise higher than I ever could have on my own.

Tenacity carried me through childhood traumas, and when I made the decision to drop out of college, it allowed me to pivot and dive head-first into a career I hadn't originally planned. But even then, it wasn't tenacity alone that gave me the courage to embrace a new path. It was the conversations with my father, the advice from mentors, and the faith of people who believed in me more than I sometimes believed in myself. These connections were lifelines in moments when self-doubt clouded my vision, and each time I leaned into them, I found the strength to keep moving forward.

The construction industry has been a true test of my tenacity but also a testament to the power of connection. As a woman without a degree, I often felt like I was fighting an uphill battle in a male-dominated field. There were moments when projects didn't go as planned, when deadlines felt overwhelming, and when imposter syndrome crept in, threatening to derail my progress. But every time I thought I might falter, I reached out to my network—whether it was a colleague, mentor, or even my father—and their guidance kept me steady. They reminded me of my capabilities when I started to question them. It was those connections that fortified my tenacity, turning each challenge into an opportunity for growth.

Living with grit isn't just about individual resilience; it's about recognizing the vital role others play in that resilience. When setbacks happen, we're often taught to "tough it out" on our own, but the truth is that no one can endure hardship entirely alone. It takes the wisdom, experience, and encouragement of others to make the journey not only bearable but transformative. The people who have lifted me up along the way have been as integral to my story as my own perseverance.

Setbacks and failures are part of the process, but so is the community that rallies around you. The resilience to get back up after being knocked down is cultivated by those who help you see that failure isn't the end—it's a stepping stone. The intention to pursue what truly matters, even if it means walking away from what doesn't serve you, is often clearer when you have trusted voices guiding you. It's about having the tenacity to keep moving forward, even when the path isn't clear, and knowing that the connections you've built will be there to support you, even when you stumble.

As I've matured in both life and career, I've learned that I don't need to have it all figured out. The people who truly care about you will remind you of this again and again. My journey has taught me that I can't carry the weight of others' expectations or the burden of past pain and still hope to grow. It's in setting boundaries and learning to say no to what doesn't align with my values that I've carved out space for what truly matters to me. And the beauty of it is that the right people—the ones who genuinely care—will respect those boundaries and cheer you on for holding firm to them.

Real fulfillment lies not in doing it all but in doing what brings you joy, growth, and purpose. It lies in surrounding yourself with people who understand the importance of this and encourage you to pursue it. My father's steady guidance, my bonus mom's unwavering support, my husband's constant encouragement, the bond with my siblings, and the professional relationships I've cultivated have all played pivotal roles in shaping who I am today. These connections have been my foundation, just as much as my own tenacity has been.

In the end, the theme of "grit" is not solely about surviving life's obstacles but about thriving despite them. Thriving comes from choosing to live intentionally, with tenacity and authenticity, but also with the understanding that you don't have to do it alone. The right connections— whether family, friends, or mentors—are as essential as the grit itself. They are the ones who help you stay grounded in moments of doubt, who offer perspective when you can't see the bigger picture, and who celebrate your victories as if they were their own.

The power of connections is that they lift you when your strength wavers and remind you of your purpose when the road ahead seems unclear. Grit gives us the strength to push through, but it's the people we connect with who provide the encouragement, the resources, and the love to keep going. My journey is proof that while you can't have it all, you can have the right people by your side—and that makes all the difference.

Living with grit means recognizing the importance of these connections, because no one succeeds alone. My dad and bonus mom gave me the foundation I needed to thrive, just as the network I've built in the industry has helped me grow. The truth is, resilience, intention, and tenacity are essential, but they flourish when supported by strong, meaningful connections. My career has taught me that success isn't just about working hard—it's about cultivating relationships, knowing when to rely on others, and recognizing the value of community.

For me, living well with grit is a blend of tenacity, resilience, intention, and connection. It's about understanding that while I may be capable of great things on my own, I am capable of even greater things with the support of others. The connections I've made have shaped the person I've become, and they continue to shape the person I am becoming. And that, above all else, is what living well with grit truly means.

Elizabeth Knight, though everyone calls her Eli, is a wife, mother of two spirited children—Remy and Rhoen—and a passionate connection crafter in the construction industry.

Raised between the shores of Gulf Shores, Alabama, and the industrial heart of Granite City, Illinois, Eli's path is fueled by her drive to break barriers. She began her journey in the construction industry at icon Mechanical at 19, later exploring the general contracting side before returning to her roots.

Eli has always embraced connection—whether through conversation or her commitment to empowering women. Known for her boundless energy and being the one who always got "Excessively Talks" on her report card, she now uses that voice to craft meaningful connections, helping others find their unique place in the industry. Eli is driven by the belief that through connection, we can build bridges where none existed and break down the walls that limit us..

Please scan the QR code to connect with this author.

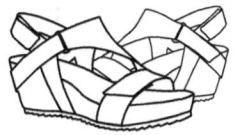

Deb Cox

The Diagnosis That Rewrote My Life's Purpose

"And so, lifting as we climb, onward and upward we go, struggling and striving, and hoping that the buds and blossoms of our desires will burst into glorious fruition 'ere long."
– Mary Church Terrell

For years, I had been struggling with persistent pain that was unexplained. Visit after visit, doctors could not find a reason. After a while, a few even questioned if I was even in pain at all. Being prescribed everything from pain pills and muscle relaxers to steroids and antidepressants, having someone think that it was "all in my head" seemed to make my suffering even more intense. There were times that I started to question my own sanity while feeling like my body was betraying me. Then, finally, the day came.

In the summer of 2009, I was diagnosed with Systemic Lupus Erythematosus (SLE). It was a mouthful, but finally, I could put a name to my pain. I began to do all the research on lupus I could. I learned that lupus is an incurable disease that occurs when the immune system attacks its own healthy tissues and organs. It could affect my skin, joints, kidneys, and heart. Lupus is a chronic and often disabling autoimmune disease in which the sufferer experiences intense fatigue and exhaustion, joint pains, thinking and memory problems, and skin rashes. All of which I had been going through for many years.

I also found that it could take almost six years after the onset of symptoms to receive a lupus diagnosis. And Black women were disproportionately affected by this disease. It may seem odd to hear, but hearing this diagnosis brought me a great deal of relief. First, it confirmed I was not crazy! And secondly, I received validation that the pain that had plagued me for over five years was real. Not only did I set out on my healing journey, but this day also began a journey that would hold a much deeper calling for me.

As if being a single parent of two college students and living with the challenges of a chronic disease were not enough, I made the decision to fulfill a lifelong dream of going back to college. It wasn't just about earning a degree but more about reclaiming my power, setting an example for my children, and proving to myself that it's never too late to follow your dreams.

Returning to school as a busy adult was not easy. Balancing a full-time career, going to university full-time, raising two children, and managing my health required every ounce of strength I could find. There were days when the pain was so overwhelming that it took all my willpower just to get out of bed. However, it was during these times of struggle that I found my resilience. My strength was in facing every obstacle with grace, determination, and belief in my ability to succeed.

During my journey I found a renewed passion not only for achieving my own goals but for helping other women to do the same. I knew that if I could navigate the challenges of being a single parent, a student, and a lupus warrior, I could empower other women to reach their career and life goals as well. My mission became clear. I wanted to uplift women, be their champion, and demonstrate how to have the strength to overcome any obstacle in their path.

As a Certified Personal and Executive Coach, I've dedicated myself to this mission. Every day, I work with women who, like me, have faced or are facing their own battles. Balancing a career with children, returning to school, or upskilling, or finding the courage to pursue a better life for themselves. I've seen the amazing transformation that occurs when a woman realizes her worth, taps into her potential, and takes control of her future.

A Ghanaian scholar said, "If you educate a man, you educate an individual, but if you educate a woman, you educate a nation." There's a unique power when women uplift women. It can change lives, communities, and generations. My role as a coach is not just about guiding women toward their goals but standing beside them as they navigate challenges and celebrate their wins, reminding them that they already have everything they need within them to succeed. They just must be willing to put in the work.

My passion for this work stems from my own journey. Every woman I work with is a testament to the strength, resilience, and determination that women possess. Empowering women isn't just what I do but who I am. And I'm reminded every day of the power we all hold to create the life we deserve.

I found that the grit, resilience, intention, and tenacity I had cultivated through my own challenges could be the tools that would help others find their life purpose and reach their highest potential. This fuels my passion for helping others find their way through their own challenges without excuses.

During my time of self-discovery, I was transformed. I discovered that the symbol for lupus was a butterfly. And butterflies are symbols of growth, transformation, hope, and freedom. And when I think of my transformation, I wrote this poem to describe my journey:

I was in a cocoon of self-discovery. In a chrysalis of self, I was on a journey, a winding path to discover me... How to Lead with vulnerability, speak with sensitivity, listen with curiosity... Not question my abilities... So, I decided to invest in me... I released what no longer served to embrace new possibilities. I live unapologetically and thrive in a sea of uncertainty... I've learned to practice good enough, for I am a recovering perfectionist, you see...

Someone said that I couldn't have it all. But I said I can! Because I can accomplish anything with faith, purpose, and a plan... It's courage that moves us forward, while fear only holds us back. I heard that fear stood for false evidence appearing real, so doing it scared, that's my counterattack...

*Because at the heart of the matter, the gist of it all, is that there is value in the valley, so I answered the call... To **grow** through, what I **go** through...Not always going up, sometimes going wide...Seeing every challenge as an opportunity...Trafficking in possibility is where my future lies...*

Finally learning to realize what I can see with my own real eyes...

Learning my true value, not negotiating my worth...

Pure potential, infinite possibilities for my life were unearthed...

No longer an imposter, I know my identity...It's Authenticity, I'm free to be me!

As this metamorphosis has taken place, I now emerge a butterfly...
Understanding my purpose, my path, and my why. Imparting new-
found strength and wisdom, I hope my words inspire other women to
know they can transform their own lives.

I transformed my pain into purpose and transformed my struggles into strengths. And in my work with others, I found a way to not just survive but to thrive. Living with chronic pain is a journey. One that requires more than just physical endurance. It demands that you redefine what it means to be strong, what it means to be successful, and what it means to live life fully.

Today, living well means I give what I have, even when that may not feel like enough to others. I rest without apology to honor my body's limits. I refuse to allow this disease to control my life, instead I reclaim it! Lupus is no longer a disease I suffer from but a "dis-ease" in my body that I live with.

I've learned to live my best life, not despite my pain but alongside it. My hope is to serve as an inspiration to other women, let them know that they are not alone, and that they can take back control of their lives. And most importantly, it is all of our responsibly as women to hold space, build each other up, and lift as we climb.

Deb Cox is a Certified Personal Executive Coach who uses a strength-based coaching approach rooted in positive psychology to inspire women to transform their lives. Her passion is helping women set achievable goals to reach their fullest potential in their lives and careers. She is a graduate of Saint Louis University School for Professional Studies. She has a degree in Organizational Studies with an emphasis in Industrial Organizational Psychology and is a graduate of Focus St. Louis Women in Leadership Class 78. Deb lives out her passion daily as the Director of Career Attainment at Rung for Women, a non-profit in St. Louis, Missouri, whose mission is to inspire all women to climb the economic opportunity ladder so that women are leading equitable and abundant lives. Deb resides in Ferguson, Missouri, with her amazing family—Maureen, Andrea, Wesley, and Solomon.

Please scan the QR code to connect with this author.

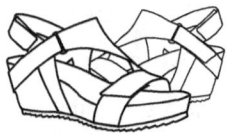

LaKricia Cox

Perseverance and Purpose

When I reflect on my life, I know that every experience I had, every mistake I made, every barrier I faced, every opportunity I had to stand up for others was shaping me and leading me to my purpose. And I cannot help but be grateful. I have learned that it does not matter how or where you start in life, what is most important is how you finish…and the people you impact along the way. I firmly believe that every single person has a purpose. We all have different journeys and are designed to accomplish different assignments, but what we contribute is critical to shaping the world around us. Our purpose may not be "grand," but could be a series of kind gestures and helpful works that nonetheless have made a difference to others. Once we begin to understand our "why," we see every step of our journey as important to our development and know there is nothing that can hinder us from achieving our destiny.

I would say my purpose began taking shape as a young girl. I was always told that I talked too much and would often get in trouble at school for speaking out of turn in class or talking too much with friends. Sometimes, my father would even pay me just to be quiet so that he could have some peace of mind! My parents separated when I was younger, and I was primarily raised by my mother. My mother had three girls, and I was the youngest. I commanded a lot of attention in my home because there was a significant age gap between me and my sisters. I was an avid listener and was often surrounded by women with strong values and opinions. Therefore, I was very comfortable speaking my mind and voicing my desires. Some of my peers described me as being bossy, but at the time, I never really understood why.

As I got a little older, I observed that not everyone was comfortable with speaking up on behalf of themselves. I made it a point to do it for them because I could not tolerate watching someone be treated unfairly. As a result, I sometimes put myself in precarious situations. I once got into a fight standing up for a girl that was being bullied by a group of boys. I was so upset because she was being attacked for trying to do what was right. So, I thought the right thing for me to do was to defend her honor. In that instance, I did not consider that this then made me the target. Another time, I was accused of being "evil" for telling the truth about a girl that was being touched inappropriately. I was told not to comment on such things and that I should be quiet. Thankfully, my mother came to my defense. I could not understand why people were so afraid of uncovering the truth, and I continued to speak out for others in high school and beyond.

During this stage in my life, I had no fear when I was speaking up for others. I remember one distinct moment when I went to the principal's office to voice my concerns about a teacher that I felt misrepresented a student. One of my classmates was absent because she had to take care of her daughter. The teacher took that opportunity to use her as an example and told the class that she would never amount to anything because she was a teen parent. I was outraged that a teacher would share such things about a student with the class. More importantly, it was incomprehensible for me to accept that my classmate's life was no longer significant or important because she had a child at a young age. After I talked to the principal, he thought it would be a good idea to share my concerns with the teacher. She and I talked things through. Even though I never knew the outcome of that discussion, I do know that she took the time to listen. This is when I first began to see the value of standing in the gap for someone and the power of using your voice to bring about change.

Being a champion for other people became my way of life. It's primarily why I went to work for mission-driven organizations. I desire to affect change and uplift my community, and I do not want to live in a world where people are written off due to poor decisions or unfortunate circumstances that they must face in life. The fact is we all make mistakes and must overcome challenges to get to where we are going. It is how we respond to challenges that will decide our future, and sometimes this involves leaning on others or our faith.

In my thirties, I became very ill. I was in so much pain that it was hard for me to even think properly or eat. I lost so much weight that people thought I was anorexic. I was suffering from a neurologic disorder, and I could not get my seizures under control. My brain was foggy, and it even affected my speech. My confidence was shaken, and for the first time, I became very concerned about what others thought of me. My voice was muted, and I began to question my very existence. It was one of the darkest periods of my life, but there was one truth that motivated me to maintain my focus and keep pursuing everything God had for me. In Jeremiah 29:11, the Lord declares, "For I know the plans I have for you, plans to prosper you and not to harm you, plans to give you hope and a future." It was leaning on this promise that kept me moving forward, even when it looked as if I was defeated. I began to do a lot of self-reflection and focus on what I could do to change my circumstances, and I got to work.

I changed my diet, which helped tremendously, and I began to think again on how to be a blessing to others. I started by addressing an injustice in my community that affected my kids' livelihood and education. I then poured myself into community projects that I thought would have even greater outcomes. As I did, I got a little stronger and my energy began to return. Likewise, with my professional career, I was not concerned with position or title but what mission I could lend myself to that could have the most impact. I began to focus more on what I could do to help other people grow and pursue their purpose and today am walking in my calling to be a preacher, teacher, intercessor, and leader in the community.

Mother Theresa once said, "I alone cannot change the world, but I can cast a stone across the waters to create many ripples." Each of us can create a ripple in our own way. Even in those crushing and frustrating moments of life, if we are walking in our purpose, they do not have to keep us down. God can and will continue to help you fulfill your purpose if you stand on His word and keep moving forward. I have learned that to live an abundant life, you must do it with love, grace, and determination. And I believe that no matter who you are, your background, failures, or the setbacks that you face, God has a plan for you!

LaKricia Cox is a speaker, teacher, intercessor, and community leader dedicated to helping people find their purpose and supporting their growth and development. She is committed to serving the community by putting love and faith into action while using her voice and influence to stand in the gap for others. As the Executive Director of Girls in the Know, she is leading the charge of empowering pre-teen and teenage girls to empower a strong sense of self through educational resources, instruction, and building a sense of community.

Please scan the QR code to connect with this author.

Linda Anderson

Urban Education GRIT

I often think of how our life paves the pathway to our destiny. Depending on limitations due to circumstances, at times, our pathways are interrupted with roadblocks, detours, and, for some, dead ends. I am honored to share how my pathway gave me the passion to teach and advocate for urban education with grit.

In elementary school, I attended St. Martin De Porres off Page Avenue on the north side of St. Louis City. All the students in the school resided in the city, and the demographics were a co-ed all-Black population. Mass was once a week, and the teachers and sisters running the school were passionate and held high expectations. My mother drove me and my brother to school every day on her way to work, and my brother and I walked to my grandmother's house once school let out. My mother and father divorced; however, they did not want to interrupt the resources from our school, community, and continued support and love from my grandmother and great-grandmother. My brother and I excelled through school, but funds were dwindling in our household, and as a single mother, there were hard choices to make...*U-turn*. So, she enrolled us in public school, and I was introduced to the arts, specifically piano.

This environment was a shift for my family, there was no connection or expectations of my mother engaging in the classroom or with the school. I mastered becoming invisible in this setting. I was not a disruption, completed all my assignments, and learned not to ask questions to prevent getting bullied by my peers. High school again was easy, I continued to soar, but my mother noticed I wasn't motivated and began to skip classes in school, so she enrolled me in what was later called the V.I.C.C. (Voluntary Interdistrict Choice Corporation) program. This program was a solution to St. Louis' efforts in desegregating our schools and promoting diversity. In this setting, I received recognition; I was in the National Honor Society and foreign language club and was introduced to different opportunities that sparked my interest in career-related positions. When it was time to apply for college, I was in the top 5 percent of my class, instead of receiving assistance with the FAFSA application and college selection, I was informed by the guidance counselor to graduate high school early...***Detour.***

I married my high school sweetheart the year after graduating high school, and we welcomed our son later that year. Life became serious, and I realized I needed to sustain a career that paid livable wages to support our family. It would take a degree and financial literacy. Balancing a management position and going to college full-time was, indeed, challenging. With determination, I was able to receive my Bachelor of Science degree in Elementary Education and dual certification in Elementary Education and Early Childhood Education...***Reroute.***

There was always a vision, there was always a plan. I read to our son every night and practiced strategies I learned from Parents As Teachers visits, and changed my managerial role at my job to work overnight shifts so I could participate in classroom jobs and be involved in the school community. I was devastated when told by the teacher he was struggling and would have to repeat kindergarten. It was explained he was immature and needed another year to mature and "catch up." I was informed of all of his deficiencies at the end of the year, and I thought, if there were a plan or preventative actions that I could take, I could do it...but what do you do to assist with immaturity in school? The strain took its toll on our family, and we divorced, and I leaned on my grandmother for support. My son did repeat kindergarten, and we moved to my grandmother's so I could have further support, and he enrolled in the public school up the street... *Sharp Turn*.

Parents As Teachers was a continued support and as my son continued to struggle in school, my daughter was reading prior to going to kindergarten. She would often sneak her brother's sight words that I placed on the refrigerator, and she remembered us reciting them daily to help with his reading. Parents As Teachers learned my daughter was reading above her level and recommended gifted testing. When I asked the school, they immediately assumed she memorized lines from a book instead of assessing her. After getting assistance from a third party, I scheduled an assessment to evaluate my daughter for gifted eligibility. She was subsequently enrolled in a public magnet school for gifted students.

At first, I was overwhelmed. The Parent Teacher Organization (PTO) at my daughter's school was dismissive of anyone outside of their distinguished groups, it was intentional, and I felt this feeling before. It was familiar, the first time being asked, "What high school did you go to?" and the clear distinctive feeling of rejection. That hurt you will never forget, the dismissiveness and exclusion when you belong leave scars that can become an infection within some people and war wounds on others... *Yield*.

Despite both of my children being enrolled in public schools, the stark differences between their educational settings amazed me. In one school setting, the air was thick with privilege, prestige, and power; my daughter's knowledge was questioned, and biases about our household were assumed, and she had to claw her way through the arrogance and pride of some of her teachers and their preconceived notions. However, the curriculum was challenging and well communicated to parents, parental engagement was expected and appreciated, and the neighborhood was inviting, everything you imagined a school would be. She was in a band and learned to play the flute in an early grade. She was in debate and Equations, a game of creative mathematics, and often went to competitions.

In contrast, my son faced the inconsistency of teachers and school closures. That early excitement that once exuded from his spirit when it was time for school became a ball of nerves, nail biting, and stomach churning; he had to learn new school communities and often dodge his daily bullies. While his sister had projects to extend her learning at home, he often had worksheets of skill and drill, which took him hours to complete. I remember the countless times I would receive calls at work from his teachers saying he needed to "pay attention." On one occasion, a teacher called after my son repeatedly complimented her sweater, incorrectly assuming his comments were an insult. I immediately asked if it glistened or changed colors, and she mentioned it was a sequence blouse. I replied, "He actually likes your shirt. It catches his attention." Sigh… WTH? (What the heck?)

My son was often excluded from field trips and other activities, and it was during this time I requested him to be tested for a learning disability. After all, I learned this was my right to request as a parent. This request went on for at least five years, and each year, I was denied–yes, denied. The pattern repeated: he enrolled in school; we'd request testing at the beginning of the year…told they needed to collect data throughout the year…at the end of the year, told he did not score low enough to get tested…school closes…begin process at new school. We lived through at least three school closings: Clay, Mitchell, and Ford. With the last school closing, I enrolled my son in a private school.

By this time, I decided to teach full-time in an urban setting, reminiscent of my elementary school experience. I chose to go where I felt my life experience would guide me to make the most impact…St. Louis Public Schools–**Reroute**.

My first year was challenging; my finances were tight, and I was expected to furnish my room (other than a desk, an old, splintered bookshelf, and the bulky teacher's desk). I imagined my classroom would come equipped with books for my classroom library…like the ones you see on Pinterest…and nice rugs for students to sit on during read-alouds, and all the color-organized cubbies to organize my different stations for students to hold small groups. Not at all! The classroom was bare, and curriculum was provided for math, reading, and science. I quickly assessed what I was provided and what I knew my students needed. There were huge gaps in resources! I spent hours filling in the holes of the curriculum, buying additional resources–like social studies, writing, grammar, and spelling and weaving that into my lessons. I loved it, I was home! I pulled from the projects my daughter was given at the "gifted school" because these were more effective in connecting the lessons and applying what they've learned. Teachers would visit my classroom to see the students engaged and working together in groups, monitoring their own progress, and holding critical discussions during our read-alouds to gauge comprehension.

I was not doing anything extraordinary; I was giving each student in my classroom the expectation that each and every one of them could accomplish their goals. That first year of teaching was necessary, science scores soared, and the school became accredited.

Urban Education GRIT

My story, journey, and pathway have taught me our brokenness is causing turmoil in our community. If the community is broken, how do we restore the community schools? If our expectations are swayed by our judgment, privilege, and unconscious biases, who is worthy of an equitable education? Close your eyes and imagine a "good" school and ask yourself:

- What do you see?
- What do the hallways look like?
- What does it sound like?

Now, what do the students look like? Urban Education GRIT is to recognize the hurt and circumstance of the urban community, mostly from systemic racist policies that have caused disinvestments in the neighborhoods. This has entered into the hallways, school yards, and classrooms of the schools. It is up to us to demand equity, fundraise to update buildings, and share research and data-driven proven strategies that will improve the quality of education for our students. They are worth it, that's our destination...***Stop***.

With well over fifteen years of experience in education and public policy, Linda strives to empower youth, educators, and the community for academic excellence, social justice, and wealth mobility. She aligns her career goals with a personal mission to revitalize disinvested communities to provide equity in education and wealth building. Linda is pursuing her Master of Public Policy Administration (MPPA) degree from the University of Missouri of St. Louis. As a member of FOCUS St. Louis Women In Leadership Cohort 76 and Washington University Women's Leadership Forum Cohort 16, she advocates for equitable and inclusive policies and practices within the organization and the wider education sector. Collaborating with different department leaders daily to structure programs, write grants, and analyze partnerships' impact on school systems, Linda also leads innovative projects. She has been able to break down silos to push forward proposals that will benefit and align with community needs. This is immensely challenging, vital work. Her drive to make a difference will have a profound and lasting impact on neighborhoods, communities, and the urban educational system.

Please scan the QR code to connect with this author.

Dawn M. Gipson

Living Well Starts Within

The year I turned 30, my mother marked time by the close of my third decade.

The topic or occasion was irrelevant. How long had it been since she and Daddy visited relatives in Tennessee? How old was the refrigerator that now needed replacing? When was the last time we had 10 inches of snow? Her answer always began the same.

"Hmm, now let me see. Dawn will be 30…"

My mother started this campaign in January. My birthday is in November.

Had it not been for the birth of my daughter, her first grandchild, she would have kept it up through December. Elyse was to be a Christmas baby, but she was born early, graciously saving me from hearing anything more about my age that year.

My daughter is 19 now, and that means two things. First, I am marking time by her twentieth birthday, which is a humorous reminder that I am more like my mother than I often think that I am.

Second, I am about to be 50. My mother passed away two years ago, so she's not here to remind me. As if I could forget.

50. Where did the time go?!?

I've come to appreciate birthdays not just as a time for celebration but as a moment of reflection as well. With 50 years in my rearview, I have a lot to think about.

Thirty years ago, I doubt that I would have imagined this life. That young woman, headed to graduate school, planned to become a graphic artist and marry her high school sweetheart. Today, I work in corporate America as an advocate for Diversity, Equity & Inclusion (DEI), and I haven't seen that boyfriend in nearly those same 30 years.

The choices that led me to where I am haven't always felt like the right ones. I questioned, doubted, and nursed fear more times than I can remember. Most times, things worked out. Other times, they didn't, and that's all right. Those situations yielded valuable lessons.

Through it all, I've been reminded of the power of connections. Meaningful bonds formed through genuine interactions. Connections require vulnerability, a level of openness that's, in a word, frightening. It's not easy to share a part of yourself, especially when you have no idea how it will be received. My list of concerns likely mirrors yours. What if I'm summarily dismissed or disregarded? The desire to avoid feeling embarrassed, empty, and exposed can keep us from trying so many things.

Oddly enough, the scariest and most rewarding connection I've made is the one I have with myself. Challenging deep-seated beliefs or the reason behind seemingly well-laid plans can lead to significant life changes. It can be uncomfortable and gut-wrenching, but whenever I've faced the discomfort, I've unlocked a new level of clarity which empowers me to be confident in my choices. My mother often said that if I did my best in any situation, I could be at peace with the outcome, regardless of how things turned out. When I share this with my daughters, I tell them to be true to themselves first. When you start there, the rest tends to fall into place. For me, self-connection is key to living well.

There have been moments in my career when self-connection provided the clarity I needed to make a pivotal decision. The first one was during my junior year in journalism school. One of my classes included a rotation on the nightly news desk of the local paper. Most evenings were uneventful. One night, a student collapsed on the basketball court and died.

The editor, who was also my professor, heard the emergency call on the police scanner and asked me to go to his dorm to investigate. She told me not to reveal his death, but she wanted me to talk with his friends. I think she wanted the article to have a personal touch instead of recounting basic facts. I disagreed. How was I going to talk to people who thought that he was still alive?

The editor threatened to give me a failing grade. Angry and uneasy, I relented. I took the long route to the dorm. When I arrived, I figured out his room number and stood in the hallway. The kids who walked past me laughing? Some of them were probably his friends. What was I supposed to say? One of his neighbors asked me if I was lost, and I told him I was looking for the student.

"Oh, he's cool!" the guy said. "Really good at basketball…"

I had never felt so sleazy in all my life. I thought about the person I wanted to be. I had no interest in sneaking around, taking advantage of future grief for a byline.

I found the dorm director, told her why I was there, and asked her to throw me out. She nodded and showed me the door. I told my editor that I had been asked to leave.

I changed my journalism emphasis from reporting to magazine design that week. I never looked back.

Most of my professional career has taken place at one company. A public relations firm hired me a year after I completed my graduate degree. My career experienced many twists and turns during my 19-year tenure. As a member of the creative department, I was, at one point or another, a graphic designer, project manager, video and event producer, and communications strategist.

It's easy to get comfortable after nearly 20 years. Most days, the job was fine. I had a competitive salary and great benefits for my family. I waved off things, little by little. The hours? The unfulfilling workload? They'll pass. Another reorganization? It's not uncommon for businesses to make changes. No promotion or raise, despite the aforementioned long hours that yielded solid, even great, results? Maybe it just wasn't my turn.

I was tired, and at first, I couldn't figure out why. Eventually, I recalled that this feeling was like that uneasiness I felt in college. My self-connection had slipped, and I wasn't fully the person I believed I was meant to be. It was time to start the job search, and my leaving was long overdue.

Turns out, the company agreed. The latest reorganization included some layoffs, and I was on the list.

As I walked out of their doors for the last time, I started to process what I was feeling. There was some sadness, to be sure, but what I felt more than anything was relief.

During the months between my old gig and the new one, I unwound my identity from the position I held at work. For far too long, I believed they were one and the same. I know now that who I am defines the role, not the other way around. My self-connection was restored, and it guided me to the next opportunity. The reason I wanted to be a journalist is because I love writing, and I love making sense of things. I now use both daily in a way that is authentic to me. As a DEI business integration partner, I help my colleagues unravel complex business challenges by looking at them through multiple lenses. When we combine a diverse range of perspectives, we can develop a strategy that has the potential to be a win for all involved.

Nurturing my self-connection with greater intention has made this latest chapter of my career the best one yet. Still, I have more work to do.

A recent experience in a leadership development program gave me an opportunity to explore my values in a way that I had never done. I believe most of us can talk about things that matter to us, but how clear are we on exactly which values influence us the most?

During the program, the moderator separated us into small groups, and each participant received a set of 30 cards that contained phrases such as fair play, respect, and dignity. We winnowed down the set to identify the phrases that were important to us. We did it bit by bit, sharing insights with our group along the way. 30 to 20. 20 to 10. In the end, I had three cards left. Family. Excellence. Personal Growth. My group discussed which of our top three values most often guided our actions.

When my turn came, I wanted to say family. I'm a wife and mother. That's what I was supposed to say, right?

I thought about that girl in college, the one who walked away from the career she thought she wanted before it even began. I remembered the person who sat still a little too long because she didn't honor her true nature.

The words I needed to say then came without hesitation.

"Personal Growth."

Acknowledging that doesn't diminish my identity in any space. I'm not less of a wife or a terrible parent because I have a growth mindset. If anything, operating from my place of clarity is what makes me an absolute badass.

We all hear the same negativity from time to time. Those thoughts and opinions that shrink our worth, seed discomfort in our abilities, and add a questioning lilt to our declarative sentences. Sometimes, this negativity comes from others. More times than not, I suspect, it comes from within. Deep down, we know these things aren't true, but we listen anyway. And we are taken further away from the connection we need to live life on our own terms.

The next time you feel uneasy, ask yourself why. What scares you more—saying no, or saying yes? Should you sit still? Move on? Whose voice are you really listening to? Be honest. The answers might surprise you.

As I move into a new decade, I will continue to care for my connected voice. Whatever choices future me will have to make may not always be easy, but they will be simple. Simply me.

Dawn Gipson is a natural-born decoder. Much of her childhood was spent at a folding card table, sifting through piles of puzzle pieces, searching through letters on a seek-and-find, or shuffling tiles on a Scrabble board.

She's applied her analytic sensibilities to several disciplines, including graphic design, event and video production, and strategic communications. Currently working as a Diversity, Equity, and Inclusion Business Partner for a Fortune 25 company, she works with internal teams to shape culture, policies, and processes that empower team members to be their best.

Dawn earned her Bachelor of Journalism from the University of Missouri-Columbia and her Master of Fine Arts from the University of Illinois Chicago.

An active member of her community, Dawn is the chair of the St. Louis Delta Foundation, a charitable organization for youth programs, and a board member for both FOCUS St. Louis and the St. Louis Forum, organizations that promote professional development and civic leadership.

Please scan the QR code to connect with this author.

Chrissy Beck

My Defining Moment

Insanity: Doing the same thing repeatedly and expecting different results.

Sometimes the biggest challenge is simply realizing you are doing that "thing" again and again, and yet here you are, in perpetual replay, longing for the day you achieve that different result. Spoiler alert: this does *not* take grit.

Like a hamster in a wheel, it took me over thirty years of repeating behaviors to realize that it was *my job* to determine my value and my purpose. I alone can create and follow the path for who I am meant to be. I am set free from comparing myself to others and determining my value solely based on how others receive and respond to me. I have found a freedom and fulfillment that has taken me further than I could have ever expected. This was not an easy lesson to come by—but rather a painful, necessary one.

I was taught from an early age that the way to feel truly seen and praised was through remarkable achievements. I was the youngest of three and probably the most average. I was not super smart or sporty. I was a well-behaved and an easy kid. This meant that my accomplishments and I did not feel naturally seen by my parents. They are not "cheerleader" kind of people, so if I wanted to stand out among my brothers, I either had to cause a ruckus (not the kind of attention I was looking for) or work hard to impress my parents. They always had high expectations and standards, which made impressing them rare—still, I would persist. I was always sure to sneak in the good news of the day if I rocked a test or was chosen for a new school role, always hoping for a warm hug with a sincere, "You work so hard, and we are so proud of you."

Now let me pause because I want to be clear: my parents are wonderful people. I am beyond blessed to be raised in their home, and I continue to cherish my relationship that I have with them. They are, and will always be, deeply loved. This story is not about them—this is about me.

Fast forward a little, and it is clear to see that with so many years of practicing the art of getting affirmation and validation from others because of my efforts, it turns out I grew up to be the definition of an "achiever." Early on in my professional career, I had just transitioned from being a middle school Spanish teacher to working in a well-recognized nonprofit, and I knew that greater things were meant for me. I wanted to learn and do more, grow in the organization, and really learn what it takes to run a business. I wanted the big office in the front corner, you know, the one with the wooden desk and large window, and nothing was going to stop me from achieving it. My oldest brother had told me, "You have to prove to them you are irreplaceable," and in that season, I was irreplaceable.

Things got tough personally. I started working two jobs: 80-100 hours a week, with a son in daycare and a baby on the way. Life was, quite frankly, chaotic. I would have to nap in the car in between jobs and was forced to make decisions between meeting friends for dinners and spending quality time with my son. I was in a place where I had to be ok with the fact that my significant other would leave mohawks in the grass with the lawnmower, fold the clean clothes inside out, and dishes would pile up in the sink longer than I was comfortable with because

I was too stretched to do it myself. It was a whirlwind of exhaustion, challenge, sacrifice, and hope.

Then my own personal miracle happened. The same coveted position in that front corner office opened in the nonprofit chapter across the Mississippi River. It was my boss at the time who had told me to apply. She always saw more in me than I ever could and always pushed me to uncomfortable spaces, knowing I would grow as a result. Filled with imposter syndrome, but covered head to toe in recommendations from former colleagues and a portfolio of rockstar achievements, I applied.

The first person I wanted to tell that I was offered my dream job was my mom. I called her from the parking lot, heart full of excitement and proud of the fact that this would be my fifth promotion in six years. I worked *hard* to get here—this was big. This would mean I could quit my second job. This would lead to more time with my family and friends, more time focused on being a mother, and most importantly, being able to give my best self to others again. Her response was, "Chrissy, now how do you expect to be able to run a whole organization, and you can't even run your household?"

I. Was. Crushed.

Was she right? Was I in over my head? Was I climbing the ladder too quickly? Did I learn enough in my other roles to be successful in this one? My mother knows me better than anyone else on the planet, and she doesn't think that I am capable of being successful—is that true? In that moment I let the door of self-doubt open wide and questioned every plan and path I had drawn out for myself. Every single day in that dream job that I worked so hard for, I showed up feeling inadequate and second-guessing every move and decision I made, even though I knew better than anyone else that I earned the right to be there. I lasted six months in this role before I self-sabotaged it.

I couldn't see it in the moment, but after I had time to process what happened, I was able to see clearly where things had gone wrong, and from this defining moment, I was finally able to exit my hamster wheel.

Other people's opinions are none of my business, and if taken too seriously, can ruin my future's path. I had to stop investing in other people's thoughts and opinions for me to be successful. I also learned that only I can love myself in the way that I need to be loved. To expect someone else to behave in a way that you want them to is setting them up for failure. For me to find my way off this proverbial hamster wheel of trying to achieve the love out of my parents, I knew I needed healing and radical change. I needed to get absolute clarity on who I am (not who people *want* me to be), what my priorities are (not what they think my priorities should be), and what my purpose is for being here. Then, once I knew who she was, I could love the heck out of her simply for who she is and who she is becoming.

It has been about seven years since I was terminated from my dream job, and I can sincerely say I am grateful for the growth that came from that experience. Once I was able to stop seeking approval, love, and validation from others and realized that all these things were inside me all along, I could align myself with the greater purpose meant for me. I was empowered to take control and create my future—no longer waiting on or blaming anyone else. This is my life, and I am the CEO.

That experience, paired with a whole lot of grit, empowered me to be comfortable and confident in being authentically me. I am no longer climbing a ladder to prove anything to anyone or seeking any sort of outward validation or applause from my achievements. It is mentally freeing to be able to do my everyday work and navigate interactions with colleagues, knowing that my intentions are 100 percent of the time from a good place: a place of teamwork and doing what is best, one of collaboration and support, and leading with love. No more hamster wheels for me!

I am simply just doing the work that fills my soul, and as a result, my team is stronger, our work is better, and our clients are well-loved.

I oversee the facility programs for the largest women-owned health-care company in St. Louis. I have multiple independent living communities that we have our program in, and our job is to help support our clients to keep them independent because that is when they are happiest and healthiest—physically, mentally, and emotionally. We recently had a client who came home from the hospital on hospice. I stayed late that day to make sure that the caregiver coming in during the evening shift had everything she needed to be successful. It is in those most unexpected moments that you can become so overwhelmingly blessed it takes your breath away. Over the next couple of days, I was able to watch my team serve a family with love and dignity beyond my wildest imagination. There were team members who worked long hours and were willing to work more, some who helped the family search for flights so that loved ones could make it to town in time to say goodbyes, some who made trips to the store and picked up snacks and drinks so that the family could focus on just being together, and so much more.

After the client passed away, I got an email:

"...I am honored that her family and she herself continued to trust us to provide excellent services throughout her time here. And I am so pleased by the attention we provided—I know that we made a difference to her and to her family by the amount of caring, compassion, and genuine love we exhibited. We have a wonderful team here and I am proud to be on an exemplary team committed to providing stellar care."

If that is the kind of impact I can make by doing my heart's work with the freedom of living authentically me—then I am here for it, and it is my duty to help others get there too.

Chrissy Beck is a catalyst, advocate, and people builder dedicated to building safe and wholehearted communities that allow others to thrive. She is an experienced nonprofit executive turned healthcare senior leader with expertise in driving organizational success and devotion to creating cultures of high performers with a passion for people.

A lifelong learner, her portfolio includes serving on the Board of Directors for Promise Community Homes, which provides affordable housing for adults with intellectual and developmental disabilities, graduation from Focus St. Louis Women in Leadership, and service to the Board of Directors for Immigrant and Refugee Women's Program.

Chrissy is currently employed with AW Healthcare, the largest female owned enterprise, serving St. Louis for over 20 years. She oversees the facility program in over nine independent living communities. As a result of this program, older adults can stay independent, where we know they are healthier mentally, physically, and emotionally.

Please scan the QR code to connect with this author.

Karen Jarrett Dupske

Go with Her Plan

"Cancer doesn't know what it's dealing with." That was my response to my first oncologist when he told me I would need to take six months off to complete my course of chemo for stage 4 non-Hodgkin's lymphoma, which I didn't know what I was dealing with. I told him I'd been working 70-75 hours a week and was willing to cut down to 40 because that was 20 hours for a normal person. He asked my then 18-year-old daughter, Lexi, "Is she always like this?" Lexi's reply, "Yes. It's just better to go with her plan." That was November 25, 2015.

My "plan" included using humor to deal with this most unwelcome diagnosis. Hearing that word "cancer" for the first time—and yes, this was only the first time of many—is soul-shaking. Lexi was 18, a senior in high school. Losing this battle and the ones that followed was not an option. Our lives were changed forever, but through it all, we became stronger and closer. My faith kept me sure that we were going to come through this.

I was guided to an organization called Cancer Support Community. I walked in three days after my diagnosis and found an organization that would support not only me but my family and friends as well. They provided Lexi and me with guidance on living through cancer, a safe, healthy outlet to deal with our fears and frustrations, words that we often couldn't express to each other. The Families Connect program helped us find our way, along with providing both of us outlets to vent and cry. I had no idea what a huge role this organization would play in our lives for years to come. I have become a member of the board and an evangelist for this amazing organization. They have provided so much support for me and my family over the years.

Chemo was hard on so many fronts. There was the sickness, the fatigue, and then the side effects, which included congestive heart failure, kidney damage, liver damage, and the decimation of my immune system. "Chemo brain" is real. To this day, I can't remember last names easily. I was blessed not to lose my hair...I know, a vain thing to be worried about with a life-threatening diagnosis, but it was a real fear. I did six months of chemo and thirteen months of maintenance treatments. They finally stopped the treatments because my immune system was so damaged that it took nine months for my body to shake a simple respiratory infection. I fell asleep mid-sentence so frequently in the evening that Lexi started keeping a notebook and pen on the couch so she could write down where we were in a conversation when I fell asleep, not knowing if I'd wake up in five minutes or an hour. My sense of taste was drastically changed. My favorite steak tasted like cardboard. We ate so much chicken and fish that Lexi feared we were going to sprout feathers or fins. Through it all, this 18-year-old turned into my caretaker and best friend. I couldn't have survived this without her.

My co-workers at Daugherty Business Solutions became my family. They made sure I was hydrated, eating, and sticking to that 40-hour work week I'd committed to. They covered for me in meetings, and when I was too sick to come into work, they brought me a sherpa blanket at home because I was always cold. They offered weekly to run errands for me. I didn't understand it at the time, but they needed that more than I did. They felt helpless and wanted to do something for me. I wished I'd accepted more help. I explained to them later that every time I accepted help, I felt like I was losing a bit of myself. I've gotten over that in the last few years. I felt so much support from Daugherty. They supported fundraisers for cancer, sent notes of encouragement, and, over the years, have provided laughter, meals, visits, and more love than I could have ever expected.

My friends Jessica and Laurie have made hospital visits, home visits, and attended my bell-ringing days. Jessica even rebuilt my retaining wall when I was too weak to do so.

After doing my first Relay for Life, I sent my CEO, Ron Daugherty, a thank you email for his donation. I was surprised to get a note back asking me how I was doing and, most of all, how the company was treating me throughout my journey. That doesn't happen anymore, especially in a company where they only make money from consultants doing billable work. When I cut my hours, it cut their revenue. Yes, I'm only one consultant, but everyone has an impact. Throughout all my five, yes five, cancer diagnoses, I have never had anyone at Daugherty be concerned about anything but my health and how they can help me. They've sent flowers, gifts, and visited me in the hospital and at home. In addition, they have provided me with the most outstanding healthcare. I would have been financially ruined multiple times without them. Daugherty continues to support the cancer organizations and events that mean so much to me.

I have received five separate diagnoses. The word cancer doesn't create fear in me like it used to. It makes me angry; it makes me frustrated and sometimes destroys the best-laid plans. Lexi and I had to cancel her graduation trip to Paris. It impacted my daughter's wedding to her amazing husband Travis, who was mortified the first time he heard me tell a cancer joke. My worst experience came in October of 2023, just two months after surgery for my second diagnosis with cervical cancer. A few days before Lexi gave birth to my fabulous grandson, Easton, I was told I had breast cancer and would need surgery. I couldn't ruin this beautiful time in their lives with this awful news. I had genetic testing, which came back negative, so I could at least tell Lexi that we didn't have to worry about the BRCA gene.

After five surgeries, nearly dying from sepsis, and three and a half months of short-term disability, I went through 16 radiation treatments. I was determined that I was going to survive this. There was no other option. I knew my daughter would be fine, but I would be damned if I would die before taking my grandson on a memory-making trip to Disney. I made it through and rang the bell yet again, and I was determined to restart my life.

The first week of July 2024 I re-created my online dating profile. A week later, out of the blue, I received a message from what seemed to be a nice guy who was actually looking for a real relationship. I so underestimated him—in a good way. Dan and I met, and I came clean about my cancer history on our first date. I gave him a free pass to make a run for the door, but he didn't flinch. As the next few weeks went on, he listened to me talk about the issues I had with my new body and what I'd been through. He was kind, understanding, and not put off by the humor I used to deal with my health history.

In the meantime, I was back at work and between consulting projects. When you come back to work, people mistakenly think you are "back to normal." They don't understand it's a new normal. One filled with anxiety over your new body, your reduced energy levels, and memory issues. As survivors, we try to keep all of that hidden. You try to make everyone think you are the same person you were before. It's a constant battle.

A couple of weeks after coming back to work, I got a message from one of our engagement managers who had a high-visibility consulting role open up at a newer client. I had a 10-minute call with the client, trying to sound positive, ready to take on the world, and most importantly, not anywhere near as exhausted as I really felt. An hour later, I found out they wanted me to start in two days. I was terrified. I didn't know how I was going to be that person on the phone for eight hours a day. Radiation exhaustion is real, and I hadn't been able to stay awake all day in months. I didn't know how I was going to take on the type of intense, highly visible role that previously came so easily. I only had two days to prepare. It was rough, but I kept hearing my dad's voice in my ear "You can achieve anything if you want it bad enough." I forced my way through the days, refusing to give in, and most of the time, when I came home, it was all I could do to take my dogs outside and feed them before I fell asleep. Weekends were all about sleep and recovering from the week. On nights Dan and I would go out, I would have to take multiple naps during the day. Gradually, over the first two months back, I started getting my energy back. I knew if I just kept going, I would be ok. Three months later, I'm still not at 100 percent, but I know I can do it. I have done it. I have survived and thrived.

Four weeks after starting with my new client, I got a call from my doctor. My pap smear came back bad. I was dealing with cervical cancer for the third time. Dan has a fantastic but challenging career and a lot of family obligations. He didn't need this. I was actually looking at ending this new relationship when my friend Melisa told me to let him make the decision. I went to his house and laid out the situation, along with the most likely scenario for treatment. He didn't blink. As I sat on his couch crying, he simply put his arm around me and told me that I would be ok and we would get through this. Yes, he used the word "we." He went with me for my biopsy and took care of me that night when I was in pain and exhausted. He is the calm to my storm. Two weeks later, I got a call from my doctor. The original diagnosis was wrong. The test was a false positive. My cancer wasn't back.

I've heard my whole life that God will never give me more than I am capable of. Sometimes I think He has a whole lot more confidence in me than I do. I am going to be ok. In fact, those couple of days off might best be used for starting to plan that trip to Disney that we are taking in two years, along with renewing my passport for trips to Paris and Greece that are at the top of my bucket list. I believe that God is telling me that I have a lot more to do before I am done here. I'd better get moving.

Karen Jarrett Dupske is a Principal Consultant and client champion at Daugherty Business Solutions and a graduate of the Washington University School of Engineering. She is a four-time cancer survivor and relentless advocate for cancer-fighting organizations, serving on multiple committees for the American Cancer Society and the Board of Directors at Cancer Support Community of Greater St. Louis, as well as the United Way of Greater St. Louis.

Karen has a passion for working with underserved youth interested in STEM careers and helped create the Access Point program at Daugherty. She is a mom to Lexi, dog mom to two crazy Westies (Bentley and Beemer), enthusiastic "Gigi" to Easton (her grandson), an obsessive UGA football fan (Go Dawgs!), and a voracious reader. Her bucket list includes trips to Paris and Kythera, Greece, where her family is from.

Please scan the QR code to connect with this author.

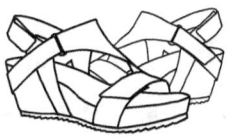

Shannon Durio

Running Toward Renewal

It was 9 p.m. on a Tuesday, and I finally collapsed onto the couch after wrangling the kids into bed. The TV remote in one hand, a glass of wine in the other—this was my nightly routine. But as soon as I settled in, my eyelids started to droop.

"Wake up! You've been waiting for this moment all day," I thought.

My day had begun entirely too early after a night of tossing and turning. It was spring of 2020, and "shelter-in-place" orders had begun to fray every last nerve. Cooped up at home with a ten-year-old, a three-year-old with developmental and speech delays, and two dogs had me rattled. My husband worked the night shift as an essential worker, which meant he slept during the day, leaving me to try and keep the aforementioned crew quiet in our tiny home as we all logged in to our respective virtual workspaces. Three-year-olds with IEPs on Zoom—what an experience.

At the time, I was the executive director of a small nonprofit organization. The pressure to keep things afloat during a pandemic was crushing. Raising money, making payroll—people's lives depended on it. Every day, I logged into my laptop before sunrise to start working, knowing that once the kids were awake, I would have to juggle virtual school and family life. By the time their bedtime rolled around, we were all exhausted.

Yet, instead of falling into bed myself, I crawled to my spot on the couch and grabbed my bottle of wine. "I deserve some 'Me Time,'" I told myself. "I earned this!" One glass, two glasses … three? Three episodes, four episodes … five? It was usually after midnight when I finally surrendered to sleep.

This 'Me Time' mantra was not unique to me. Moms everywhere spent their days trying to meet every need, wearing the parent, teacher, nurse, coach, and employee hats, sometimes all at once. A little uninterrupted time at night to just *chill* without anyone depending on us seemed warranted. No matter that I woke up every morning bleary-eyed and battling a headache, making it harder to be productive—and sane—the rest of the day.

For me, the pandemic never seemed like one breaking point but more of a breaking season. The pressure was closing in, and I was anxiously searching for refuge. I had settled for quick fixes that allowed me to momentarily escape, but the "peace" was short-lived.

Catching a glance of my reflection in the mirror one morning, I stopped in my tracks. I hardly recognized myself; stress, fatigue, and the remnants of a hangover lined my face, disappointment reflected in my eyes. A thought crossed my mind:

"Why am I settling for this version of myself?"

I had always struggled to realize my intrinsic worth, but now the consequences of that were evident in my deteriorating health. Tears sprang to my eyes when I thought about the example I was setting for my kids—specifically, my daughter. The world (social media, especially) sets painfully unrealistic expectations for young girls. I wanted her to know she was created by God with a purpose and to believe she was strong and capable. I had a responsibility to model that for her.

But first, I needed to believe it about myself—and that would take more than one of the quick-fix solutions I'd been turning to for years.

I contemplated my new existential crisis, naming all the reasons why I was unqualified to uncover the best version of myself. Then I heard my husband's familiar refrain in my head: "Excuse me, lady. I don't let anyone talk trash about my wife. That includes you. So, stop it."

I smiled a real smile for the first time in months. Maybe I *could* do this.

But … where do I start?

Coincidentally, just before the onset of the pandemic, I had challenged my dad to train for a half marathon with me. Neither of us were distance runners, but we both enjoyed a nice, easy 3-mile jog on occasion. He agreed, so we had been long-distance "training partners" for a few months, him in South Dakota and me in St. Louis. But if running was going to be my catalyst for change, I needed to put some structure around it.

We signed up for a race, giving me an immediate, measurable goal to work toward. But improving my overall health—physically, spiritually, and mentally—was the bigger goal.

It didn't take long to see the obstacles in my way: a taxing job, social isolation, a lack of self-confidence, sleep deprivation, and alcohol. As it turns out, getting up early to run after a wine-fueled Netflix binge and only four hours of restless shut-eye is rough.

I suppose some people are able to identify a challenge and quit their vices and bad habits cold turkey, but that was not me. It was a slow, often grueling process that required me to push myself out of my comfort zone to grow.

Even the introvert in me recognized that I couldn't do this alone. I needed people to walk alongside me on this journey.

I needed community.

Although 800+ miles away in South Dakota, my dad became a primary source of support. His encouragement was unwavering. After particularly hard runs, he reminded me everyone needs grace in moments of struggle. We started using "#GraceCrew" at the end of our messages, serving as a reminder that we were in this together.

As the world began to open up again, I was thrilled to regain a routine I'd lost during the pandemic: church. My faith has always played a foundational role in my life. But on my quest to rebuild my community, I found myself achingly lonely at the megachurch we had attended for nearly a decade. Its vast size allowed me to slip in and out each Sunday without anyone noticing. I was comfortably invisible.

One morning, during a coffee meeting with a longtime donor, he mentioned that his cousin was a pastor at a local church in St. Louis. "I'm personally agnostic, so I don't attend," he told me. "But he's a great guy, and the church seems to be growing."

I visited the following Sunday. From the moment I walked through the doors until I got to my car afterward, I was overcome with emotion. It was a smaller, incredibly diverse church where the love was palpable and the smiles genuine. It felt like home. This is what church is supposed to feel like. I still smile when I think about how God used an agnostic person to draw me closer to Him.

With renewed faith and a growing support system, I began to see tangible progress. My dad and I completed our half marathon with #GraceCrew printed on our race shirts, symbolizing the strength in our shared journey! But I kept running beyond that race. It wasn't just about physical fitness anymore. It was about reclaiming my life.

As my fortieth birthday approached, my husband floated the idea of a bucket list trip to Hawaii. In a moment of either thoughtful reflection or sheer idiocy (possibly both), I told him I would rather take the next step in my health journey and invest in a running coach for a year. The new goal: to train for a *full* marathon before I turned forty.

To his credit, he only allowed his jaw to hit the floor for a brief second before he agreed to support my crazy plan. For more than a decade, he had walked with me through my seasons of crippling self-doubt and fear of inadequacy. That night, there was a flicker of a fire in my eyes, a hope that maybe—just maybe—I could achieve something that had once seemed like a pipe dream. He was all in for me, as always.

One morning, after a run, I met a woman at the trailhead. As we chatted, I found out she was an accomplished local running coach. Coincidence? I'd say divine intervention. Meeting Jacqueline Sommer that day and hiring her shortly thereafter changed my life. I knew that my health was a worthwhile investment—especially when I considered all the money I threw away on alcohol and Starbucks for so many years!

Accountability in the process.

Jacqueline was worth every penny. As a busy mom herself, she understood my scheduling challenges and created weekly plans that pushed me to the next level. We talked every day about what went well, what didn't, and how I could adjust to improve. One day at a time. She was an extension of my #GraceCrew.

It was a grind. For a full year, I ran five days a week. Training in St. Louis year-round is a special kind of hell. I ran in temperatures below zero and over 100 degrees, rain, snow, or shine, and at 5 a.m. or 5 p.m., depending on my schedule. I hired babysitters for the days I had long runs and my husband was at work. I ran on vacation and during business travel. In that year of training, I only missed six workouts. An accountability partner helped reframe my internal narrative—I felt strong and capable.

One of the most significant things I learned from Jacqueline was to listen and be kind to my body. With this in mind, I overhauled my evening routine, knowing that good sleep hygiene was critical to my overall health. I swapped cabernet for Sleepytime Tea. I bought comfortable pajamas and renewed my library membership and picked up books instead of the TV remote. (Can we just talk about the magic of libraries? Free books!) Most nights, I was in bed before 9 p.m., helping regulate my sleep patterns to support physical and emotional recovery.

Faith and friendship.

Possibly the most profound part of my health journey was the spiritual renewal I experienced. My pastor Brent Roam says church is where we "learn in rows (sitting shoulder-to-shoulder during a service) and grow in circles (gathering in small groups)." I'd spent my life in the pews but was finally ready for the people. I took a leap of faith …

And wouldn't you know it, the smaller community I found at my church was transformational. I plugged into two Life Groups and built connections with women of all ages and ethnicities, from all walks of life. We learned to do life together. We forged genuine bonds as we served together, studied Scripture, prayed, and got real with one another. In one group, I was vulnerable about my struggle to navigate social settings without alcohol. Their response brought me to tears: several shared that they, too, faced similar challenges, and then they planned group "Mocktail Outings" as a supportive and inclusive alternative. It was a beautiful expression of how friendship is found at the intersection of health and healing.

The return on investment.

Three weeks before I turned 40, I completed my full marathon. It was as challenging and rewarding as I imagined it would be. At mile 21, I was feeling the burn. Everything hurt. I turned for the final 5-mile stretch and was blasted by relentless 30+ mph headwinds. After a moment of panic, I took a deep breath. Jacqueline's pre-race encouragement flew through my mind: "It will be hard. But you have already proved you can do hard things. Dig deep!" I could almost hear my dad yelling, "It's just a little resistance training! You've got this!" I could feel the strength of my #GraceCrew, even on the stormy race route.

I said a quick prayer and gave it everything I had, pulling from a reservoir of faith and confidence I'd spent years building until I finished the race. When I saw my kids' smiles at the finish line, I knew then that the generational cycle of fear and self-doubt stopped with me.

Crossing the marathon finish line was one of the proudest moments of my life, but the real victory was in the journey. I developed a framework for healthy living rooted in community, accountability, and faith, which has changed the way I show up every day.

2 Corinthians 12:9-10 (NIV): "*But he said to me, 'My grace is sufficient for you, for my power is made perfect in weakness.' Therefore, I will boast all the more gladly about my weaknesses, so that Christ's power may rest on me. That is why, for Christ's sake, I delight in weaknesses, in insults, in hardships, in persecutions, in difficulties. For when I am weak, then I am strong.*"

Shannon Durio is a dynamic fundraising executive with 20 years of experience turning passion into action in the nonprofit sector. She has made her mark in frontline fundraising roles, from national organizations like the American Cancer Society and March of Dimes to community-centered groups such as Concordance, the Foster & Adoptive Care Coalition, Prison Performing Arts, and FamilyForward.

For Shannon, fundraising is more than just a job—it's a powerful way to connect people with opportunities that address critical needs and foster transformative change within communities. Currently, she brings her expertise to her role as Vice President of Development at We Raise Foundation, supporting Christian organizations and leaders working at the intersection of poverty, violence, and inequality. When she's not championing causes or volunteering her time, Shannon treasures family time, the running trail, and the occasional peaceful moment on the couch with a good book.

Please scan the QR code to connect with this author.

April Planck

Not Good Enough, Says Who?

Have you ever wondered if you are good enough? Well, I have. Am I a good enough mother, a good enough provider, a good enough friend, leader, or mentor? Who decides what good enough looks like? How is it measured? Why do we let others decide what good enough means for us? Will I *ever* be good enough?

These thoughts are traumatizing, debilitating, often life-altering, and unfortunately, largely self-inflicted. When you see someone succeeding—doing or being the thing you strive to be doing—does the voice in your head say, "Girl, you got this. You can do that!" or do you hear, "You're good, but you're not *that* good." For many of us, including myself, it's the latter. Why do we feel this way, and better yet, how do we flip the narrative to be our own advocate and our own cheerleader?

Who decides what good enough looks like for me? *I do!* Why do I let others decide for me? Because I value the opinions of others more than I value my own. I said it. It hurts, but it's true. I crave constant validation. Nothing makes me feel more confident than having someone I admire or respect tell me that I *am* doing something right. Getting that compliment or validation is a trigger that allows me to see that accomplishment in myself and seemingly gives me permission to start measuring myself.

"Maybe I *am* good at this thing; could it be true?" We only start to value ourselves when we hear how valuable we are to others.

In 2007, I was a 32-year-old mother of three boys, ages one to eleven, and a construction project manager for a life safety provider, and I loved it. I was good at it. People said so. Not only was I the first project manager they had ever hired, but also a female, which was very rare in the industry at that time. Even though I knew this was true and it meant something, it didn't make me feel good enough. I'd been in the industry for years and just really wasn't going anywhere. I knew I could and should be doing much more. I desperately wanted to move up, and I dreamt of getting a leadership title. It was all about that title to me. If I got the title, that would mean I had earned the respect I deserved. Maybe I would feel good enough? I was already well respected on the team, already acting as if, and carrying on as if, I was in the leadership position. I was beyond passionate about the success of my team and company, and I deserved it. Even though I deserved it, had all the skills, more experience than most, the right temperament, and the respect of my peers, I still didn't believe I was good enough. Because I didn't believe in myself, I allowed another to take a job I knew I deserved. Unfortunately, I wouldn't get another opportunity at this role for five years.

I remember that moment like it was yesterday. It defined my career at that point and the livelihood of my family. I had to do something so I wouldn't sabotage myself again. I met all the job requirements, but I lacked the self-confidence in my ability to stand up for myself. I convinced myself that I had to be better, not just good enough, but better than everyone else so that I might be worthy.

My plan for personal *growth* included getting a degree, getting outside of my comfort zone, and generally just working my ass off. I enrolled in a full-time schedule of online college courses in Construction Management, half of which I felt like I could teach. Nonetheless, the degree was something that I allowed to hold me back. I had to get it. It was time. I worked full-time with three young kids, studied and completed coursework in the middle of the night and on weekends, and got the degree in two years. Was this good enough? I didn't know, but it didn't hurt.

After completing my degree, I joined every construction industry association and organization that I could find and became as active as I could. This is the thing that got me out of my introvert's comfort zone. Unknown at the time, the knowledge and networking that I gained from my inclusion in industry organizations is immeasurable to this day. Words struggle to describe how these lifelong friendships and industry relationships have elevated my self-worth and confidence, not to mention the improvement of specific skills such as leadership, public speaking, and participation on a board of directors.

Lastly, in my quest to better myself, I took on the motto of never saying "*no!*" I said "yes" to everything. When it came to work, my team, my company, and the construction industry, people were going to know who I was. I wasn't giving them a choice. I was everywhere. I needed to be part of everything. I wanted to be exposed to as many new things as I could learn and meet all the players. I needed to be a better problem solver, so I jumped in to help anywhere they would let me. I convinced myself that when people knew who I was and could associate me with a job well done, I might start to be good enough.

Fast forward five years, I've gotten the Construction Management degree, and I have a very solid career and a hefty network of industry professionals and friends around me. The family is doing great, by the way. I got the leadership job and the money to go with it, and life was great. These things *did* make me feel good and accomplished but they are *not* the things that made me value myself.

I literally accomplished some great things in a few years, but I was doing great things all along and just refused to see them. I created a career out of nothing while getting married and starting my family at 21 years old. That's not "nothing." I went from admin to Assistant Project Manager in two months; that's not "nothing." I went from Assistant Project Manager to full-fledged Project Manager, responsible for millions of dollars of military projects in two years. Also, not "nothing." I was one of the youngest project managers around town and was known for it; again, not "nothing." Finally, I was promoted to be the first female Operations Manager in my region. I made it. This was the title I had to have.

Construction is a male-dominated workforce, so you can imagine how hard it is to be accepted in critical roles as a young female. I had grown up in the industry. My grandfather, whom I admired and looked up to immensely, was a custom home builder and the hardest-working guy I have ever known. I spent plenty of time with him on sites, and he never once said that it wasn't a place for me. If there was ever a thing in my life that I felt strong and confident about, it was this. No one was going to tell me that I didn't belong in this industry, in this "man's world," that I was so passionate about. Succeeding as a woman in this industry for as long as I have has taken *resilience*. It has not been easy, nor fair, at times, but that's a story for another time. I love the construction industry.

Back to my journey…Do you know what else I gained in my time bettering myself? A purpose. My plan to be better actually brought out things in myself that I didn't know were there. I found hidden strengths and talents I never saw before. I found them on my own; no one had to tell me they were there. Whoa! I found that I have a passion for mentoring others to see their strengths and achieve their goals. This passion drives me to this day. I am very *intentional* about supporting the people in my life that need it. I learned how something as simple as giving a woman a genuine compliment, and I mean genuine, can have such a profound effect on them. It doesn't hurt me to dish out true compliments to someone who needs or deserves one as often as possible. In fact, selfishly, it makes me feel great about myself. Helping someone see value in themselves makes me feel amazing. I love it; give it a try.

Don't wait for others to tell you how good you are. Tell yourself. Would you compliment someone else for doing something you do all the time? If the answer is yes, then you *are* good enough. Compliment yourself for the things you are doing well. My advice is to avoid setting boundaries regarding yourself. If you are applying for a job and aren't sure you meet all the requirements, who cares? Can you do the job? Do you know in your heart that you would slay it? Then click that apply button and go shine in the interview. You got this! Focus on the nine out of ten things you are great at and understand that you have room to grow. We all have room to grow and improve. Be *tenacious*. Believe in yourself and believe it when others believe in you.

When it comes to measuring what good looks like, be careful setting too many precise goals to accomplish. Goals are good, but it's the journey that ends up defining us. Keep an eye on the goal but keep your ears to the road. You don't want to miss the good stuff while you're traveling to your destination. Don't limit yourself by only being good enough if you do this or do that. Search out the things you are already good at and remind yourself. Confidence builds confidence, and by the way, it's contagious too. Spread the word, tell a friend, tell a stranger how good they are. Go out of your way to remind someone that they *are* good enough!

Don't expect perfection when you are already *good enough!*

For over 25 years, April Planck, CDT, CIT, has been an active leader in the construction industry and local community. She has a passion for not only leadership but also mentoring other women in the construction industry to find the success they deserve. In addition to her career with Marmic Fire and Safety, April has been a member of The National Association of Women in Construction (NAWIC) since 2012 and has served on the chapter board, including three terms as chapter president: 2015-2017, 2021-2022, and 2024-2025. April is a long-time member of the Springfield Contractors Association, Associated General Contractors of Missouri, Women of STEEL, Springfield Chamber of Commerce, and The Queen City Fraternal Order of Eagles # 3934.

In 2019, April was honored to be chosen as the Outstanding Woman in Construction. This Vesta award honors a woman who has been influential in the construction community for more than ten years.

While being a dedicated wife and mother of "My Three Sons," she co-owns Certified Appliance Repair of Springfield, alongside her husband Corey. The family enjoys going on unplanned adventures, RV camping, game nights, and horror movies.

Please scan the QR code to connect with this author.

Susan Duff

Reinventing with GRIT

I have reinvented myself through the years in different situations, in the workplace and in my personal life. As a kid and young adult, I observed and reflected a lot. After some personal growth work many years ago, I found my ability to take action. Now I am striving to balance reflection and action.

I had always thought that it would be "nice" later in my career to have my own consulting business. I'm not sure what I was thinking by "nice." Now that I've reached that stage in my life, it's a *lot* of work, yet work that I love. And it requires me to grow personally and professionally every day. Sometimes when I respond, I surprise even myself at how calm I feel despite the demands and business of being the CEO, the Chief Everything Officer. I am expanding my capacity to accept good things into my life.

I had been working hard on my business in start-up mode and had traveled to work with a team out of town. Across the street from my hotel was a day spa, and I had a free morning the day after my presentation before I flew home. I decided to treat myself, even though it was outside my budget. I made the appointment, enjoyed a luscious facial and massage, and walked back into the dressing area. I used the bathroom, and then discovered the slide lock on the big heavy metal door to this one-seater room with a toilet and sink was stuck. It would not budge. My phone and clothing were secure in my locker.

The dressing area was between two other sections of the spa: the treatment area on the left and the registration area to the right. I began pounding on the door, hoping that, at some point, someone would pass through the dressing area going from one section to the other. Eventually, someone did. When the front desk person walked through and figured out where the pounding was coming from, I yelled through the door that I was locked in the bathroom.

She sounded way more panicked than I was. Luckily for me, my flight was several hours away. She said she was going to get help. She came back, not sure what to do. I suggested sliding a business card under the door with some massage lotion on it to see if I could lubricate the lock and get it to move. Good try, no success.

The spa was inside a boutique hotel, so she called maintenance. They banged around and then knocked on a spot on the door across from the slide lock and asked me to push there to see if the door would open. No luck. They went to get tools to take the hinges off the door. After noisy attempts to no avail, a new woman arrived and slid a flathead screwdriver between the door frame and the door where the lock was. "Try it now!" she yelled from the other side of the heavy metal fireproof door. The lock slid right open, and there I was, standing in my white terrycloth spa robe and slippers looking at a couple of big, tall men, one in overalls and one in a suit and tie, the front desk clerk, and the woman who just walked up and solved the mystery with a screwdriver.

They all looked very concerned. They continued to stand there staring at me. They must have been waiting for a victim in tears who needed rescuing or for me to lash out in anger, making them into villains. I suppose they were heroes who were ready to either comfort me or calm me down. Those are the three roles of Karpman's Drama Triangle: the hero, the victim, and the villain, in this case, the stuck door.

But I was not a damsel in distress, nor angry, as I might have been in years past. I found the whole thing amusing. Finally, I said, "Thank you. Excuse me, I need to get dressed now and go to the office." After getting dressed, I went to the front desk and was told by the woman, "I am not going to charge you for your treatment." When I asked, she assured me my massage therapist would be paid. For forty minutes of standing in a bathroom, I scored a free massage and facial. I was grateful.

I used to experience all this as feeling quite magical, believing "the Universe," or something "out there" was responding to me. What I feel now is that when I give myself what I need to sustain myself *and* work hard toward my intentions, I attract what I need and what I deserve. The Universe is in me and all around. It is just goodness flowing through me. The more receptive I am to it, the more it happens. But that wasn't always how I experienced life. I've had to unlearn some automatic reactions to receive good things. How did I get here?

I grew up in what I think of as a typical dysfunctional American family. As a kid, my brother and I never lacked food, or clothes, or a roof over our heads. I learned a good work ethic and responsibility from both my parents. I got A's and B's in school. My brother and I went to school and did all the usual things kids do; rode our bikes and played with our friends.

There was just an invisible dynamic in the background called "The Drama Triangle" that I learned about in more depth in the last few years. (Karpman, S. 2014, *A Game Free Life: The New Transactional Analysis of Intimacy, Openness, and Happiness:* San Francisco. Drama Triangle Publications.) My mom, my dad, and my brother were each a point of the triangle, often arguing about something my brother did not want to do that my parents wanted him to do. Years later, he would be diagnosed with schizophrenia. I was usually on the outside of the triangle in the background. I poured myself into things that I could control, like being a good student. I also became an astute observer of the interactive dynamics of my family, as well as observing how other families of my friends and neighbors whose homes we visited were different than mine.

As I look back now, it's no wonder that I have a passion for helping organizations identify what is holding them back from functioning at their best and creating the conditions for conversations to emerge that allow for different perspectives. Family is generally our first experience with an organization. My family prepared me, without realizing it, for making astute observations of organizational dynamics, and infused me with a desire to help things function in a better way. I love creating exercises or questions that meet people where they are and allow them to discover the essence of what empowers them to be their best. I love helping people discover new ways of thinking and being and working together to accomplish more than they ever thought possible, while feeling joy and connection at work. Facilitating and designing conversations that make all the difference is what I'm about because otherwise, these conversations might never happen.

Connecting stakeholders to one another in ways that reinvent how they think together and work together improves their business results. There are some who learned excellent communication practices and now find themselves in an organization where they are not heard. Organizational change *can* happen. Like me, there are some who did not learn best practices in communication among stakeholders in their first organization. It can be learned. Science tells us that positive emotions like encouragement create forward momentum toward goals rather than negative emotions like stress or fear, but it also creates emotional well-being and healthier organizational dynamics. (Boyatzis, Richard; Smith, Melvin L., and Van Oosten, 2019, *Helping People Change*, Harvard Business Review Press.)

Living Well means working in my area of passion, organizational change. But it also means striving every day to be the person I want to be. *Living Well* means having a sense of self-agency and freedom to do what I need to do for myself. I can now be the person I am free to be, rather than reacting as if in a fairytale and playing the character of the villain, the hero, or the victim.

I had lost my dad to cancer in 2020, I moved, and in early 2023, the man I thought was my partner for life wanted his freedom. Since 2021 during the pandemic, I worked as an independent contractor facilitating classes over Zoom. As time went on, the contract I had signed felt restrictive as business opened up again and as the start-up phase of my business progressed.

The familiar feeling of a trapped victim came, thinking of the training firm as a villain. I remember a shift, feeling like a mama bear and committing to myself that *nothing* is going to stop me from building my business. I made a conscious decision to put myself first. From this decision, a fierce tenacity has grown. I gave my notice to the training firm and wound up re-negotiating my contract. And if needed, I will do it again. A different conversation makes all the difference.

From that time on, how I think about setting boundaries has changed. Instead of saying no to others, I say yes to me and my priorities first; saying no is simply a side effect. I draw boundaries with compassion. I might now say to someone who regularly asks me to rescue them, "I'm sorry you're so troubled by this, *and* I have to take care of myself, so I'm not able to help you today. How about tomorrow?"

The sense of responsibility to others that I learned in my first organization spurred my action-taking to extremes, which can feel like an endless treadmill of exhaustion and burnout. The result is a need for a major overhaul in my life every so often. Stopping to reflect on what I've learned through my actions or inaction creates future action that is purposeful. Reinventing my life regularly now sustains me instead of a radical transformation every few years.

I have a wonderful teacher, Dr. Nadya Zhexembayeva, who encourages sitting down with a cup of tea and candlelight to make reflection time enjoyable. Yet too much reflection can cause me to become an introverted and disheartened couch potato. A balance of moving back and forth between action and reflection is key to being the best I can be. The Healthy Reinvention Cycle (Reinvention Academy) is just one of the tools I use for myself and with my business clients. Everyone must find their balance with this dynamic.

Living Well means taking care of myself, creating my own experience no matter what life brings me, and being the creator rather than the victim of my personal and professional experience. (Emerald, David, 2016, The Power of TED* (*The Empowerment Dynamic). Bainbridge Island: Polaris Publishing Group.) My experiences have shown me that I can trust the process of life to provide me with the next thing on my journey when I need it. Every time I do something to protect my positive outlook and care for my well-being, I am rewarded. It's not always the easiest choice. It *is* living well.

I continuously reinvent my mindset through learning, experimenting, and reflecting. I learn as I go, allowing insights to pop into my mind instead of worrying or overthinking things. I learning as I network, meet new people, and have new conversations. I am working with companies that need to connect stakeholders with new conversations and new ways of thinking in this world of disruptions we find ourselves in. I am the CEO of my company. Not just the Chief Everything Officer, overburdened with the heaviness of responsibility. I promoted myself from the Chief Everything Officer to the Chief Empowerment Officer.

What do you want to reinvent?

Susan is the founder of Stakeholder-ology, a firm that connects stakeholders to reinvent how they think and work together to future-proof their business. She works with mid-market and growth-stage companies to help them navigate a path forward by creating the conditions for conversations to emerge that allow for different perspectives and new solutions.

Susan earned her Master's in Positive Organization Development and Change from Case Western Reserve University, Weatherhead School of Management. She holds numerous certifications and is a Certified Reinvention Practitioner by Reinvention Academy with Dr. Nadya Zhexembayeva.

Susan leverages proactive, research-based methodologies to address the pressing challenges of today's dynamic business environment. She helps companies overcome the pitfalls of fragmented efforts as they grow and to pivot to the collective mindset and culture needed in a fast-paced landscape.

Please scan the QR code to connect with this author.

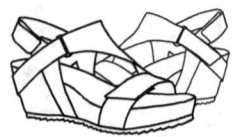

Lisa Frumhoff

Pickleball Saved My Life

I was a dormant, resigned, out-of-shape athlete by 2009, weighing over 220 pounds.

I had not competed in any sports since I won a gold medal in 1994 playing softball in the Gay Games in New York. That was also the year I started my real estate business.

To think I was turning down invitations to play pickleball. I thought the name was silly. My friend Karen helped me out by doing a huge favor for me, sitting by my side during a "trial" at a local community college. I reported a teacher for sexual harassment. Karen made only one request. "Come out and play pickleball with us." And I had to say "yes." Everything happens for a reason. A belief of mine.

Pickleball has been my pathway to rediscovering my competitive drive and has re-ignited the fire in my belly.

Playing sports was always a self-expression for me going as far back as I can remember. In seventh grade, I played soccer on a boy's team and scored goals. I loved dodgeball and kickball. It was a game changer when I was able to play girls' team sports after 1972, thanks to Title IX. In my teen years, I played softball, and I was known for being one of the toughest softball fast pitchers—versatile enough to play any position on the field—and "the cleanup hitter." A "cleanup hitter" is the fourth hitter in the batting order and is traditionally the team's most powerful hitter.

After many years of living a stagnant life in my 40s and early 50s, pickleball got me moving again and helped me start to get physically fit. I started to drop weight by moving more and trying to change my eating habits. I really didn't know how to eat properly, and I wasn't doing any strength training or weight-bearing exercising, so I looked like a "skinny fat person." My weight fluctuated between 160-180 pounds. Looking back now, I can see I never really made any changes to my body composition because I was not doing any strength training, which is critical for building lean muscle mass, strengthening our muscles, and building strong bone density for women. But what was still missing for me at this time was a healthy eating program.

In 2019, within five months, the three most significant beings in my life passed away: my 89-year-old dad and my two senior dogs, Precious (17) and Punkin (14). I turned to food for comfort. This time, before gaining all that weight back, I knew I needed to interrupt my behaviors. I also had a wake-up call and reality check. The results of my overdue blood test showed my bad cholesterol (LDL) was back over 220.

I was ready to make a change. Pickleball gave me something positive to focus on. I felt inspired to be the healthiest, best version of myself. That year, I entered my first eight-week challenge with my fitness and health coach. Being coached was where I needed to be. I needed to do the program that was designed to work, not "Lisa's" version. There was no freakin' way I wanted to take those bikini progress photos and post them online or share them with anyone, for that matter.

My Purposeful Life through Pickleball

After so many years of taking care of my aging parents and my real estate business, it was time to reconnect to myself and my life. So many of us find ourselves taking care of parents and kids. "Put the oxygen mask on yourself first," is what they always tell us before the plane takes off.

I make time for myself daily. We are worth the time it takes to learn how to eat and follow a healthy eating regimen. I put in the time to learn how to follow macros. I'm committed to setting myself up to win around eating and exercise. I make the time to prepare food and meals. It takes planning. I know I need to have my refrigerator stocked with my prepared protein and veggies. And now there are more healthy options to pick up on the go. I have learned we cannot out-exercise a bad diet. Food is 80 percent of the healthy lifestyle. The other 20 percent include strength training 3 to 5 days a week and my daily checklist. I add light cardio 5 days a week, going for a 30-minute walk. I jump 10-45 minutes on my rebounder. I add some short sprints and conditioning to help me play pickleball better. And I make sure to manage my sleep, stress, water intake, daily supplements, and the daily routine that works for me.

Having coaches in my life helps me continue to see my blind spots so that I can go beyond my own limitations and transform my life. I've dropped over 80 pounds and over 80 inches around my body. I have to make a commitment to myself and keep my word to myself.

With that said, I also know I need community and support around me. My muscle memory has less years of living with these new healthy behaviors. Whether I feel like it or not, regardless of motivation, the key is keeping my promise to myself. Consistency. Practice. Doing things I don't necessarily like all the time. Putting in the work to be the healthiest version of myself and to be the best pickleball player I can be. Having my "why" in life.

I've been able to compete at pickleball at a level that has been incredibly thrilling and life-altering Playing and coaching pickleball are a few of my happy places.

I was playing singles in the gold medal match in the Regional Pickle-ball Championship with a goal to win a golden ticket and qualify for the National Pickleball Championships. The rain delay was on and off, it was an unusually chilly 60 degrees on Memorial Day weekend. My shoulders ached from a fall I took that morning. I was distracted because everyone watching us happened to be my opponent's friends from Oklahoma, and they were cheering for her. Even the referee was from Oklahoma, which contributed to me being self-defeated in my head.

I had been undefeated heading into the finals. But my mindset was in the wrong place. I kept thinking about the points I was missing, which only made it worse. I started fearing missing my serve, and no mystery, I got a bad case of the "yips," which is slang for "a state of nervous tension affecting an athlete in the performance of a crucial action." Before I knew it, I had lost two games to my opponent and now we were tied. The winner would be determined by one final game to 15 points. We had some long, hard-fought rallies, but I found myself down 14 to 8.

My opponent was serving, and I knew that if she won the point, she would win the match. I strategically called my last time out. My mantra before every serve: "Lisa, the only point that matters is this one point right here. Nothing in the past, nothing in the future." Everything got quiet. She served the ball, we played a long rally, I ran down every ball and I won the rally. Now it was my chance to serve and win points. I repeated my mantra in my head before each of my serves and won one point at a time to win the match 16-14. I earned my first Golden Ticket to the National Pickleball Championships, and that year, I won 4th place in singles at nationals. I have competed in Nationals for three years.

At 60 years young I feel in the best shape and condition in my life. I embrace and love my healthy lifestyle that allows me to be active, play and coach Pickleball, work my real estate business, create my clay Udu drums and artwork, enjoy my family and friends, and continue to transform myself and my life.

Here is my secret recipe for my success to transform my life.

Transform

Metamorphosis. To make a thorough or dramatic change in the form, appearance, or character of. A mystery and a miracle.

Tenacity

The quality or fact of being very determined. Persistent.

Being coachable. No fat-shaming myself. Learning to notice my thoughts quickly. What we resist persists. The more I resisted being with myself in the size 18 clothing I was wearing, the harder it seemed to make any change. Being with and loving myself exactly as I am is always the place to start. This opened the pathway for me to use these progress photos to empower myself, a tool that helps us see the transformation in our bodies, even when it doesn't show on the scale. I purchased "too small of a bikini" so I could "shrink" into it. These photos are a very important part of my routine and can remain private. Throughout this process, I've gained courage, strength, and confidence.

Resilience

"The capacity to withstand or to recover quickly from difficulties; toughness."

We all have our mountains to climb. When the pandemic hit, I had been six months into my fitness and wellness routine, which helped me navigate a little better with the food and exercise part. Losing weight is hard enough. Keeping it off presents its own challenges. Between 80 and 85 percent of those who lose a large amount of weight regain it. I was back up to 160 pounds by March 2024. No mystery. I stopped doing the things that I had done the first time to reach success in my goals. I went back to my old habits. Which got me the same old results. This time, on top of having to do the work again, I had to stop making myself wrong for going backward.

Accountability

"Accountability entails your actions and their effects."

A critical part of my success has been accountability, not only to myself but also to my coach, Stephanie, and to my community, including my Team Warrior Fitness group. We are unstoppable warriors. I got tired of hearing my excuses. It required me to do the work. Period. I knew how much work it took to drop those final 25 pounds the first time. I felt empowered when I took responsibility for my actions that put on those 25 pounds. When I hear any hints of me sounding like a victim, I catch myself. I take back my power by owning it. If it's to be, it's up to me (another mantra of mine).

Being accountable to a coach takes us to a whole new level of results. Having a coach has always helped me produce breakthrough results in my life, like being an All-America soccer goalkeeper. A great coach can help us see what our blind spots are, and that's where the miracles happen.

Nutrition

Everyone seems to know how to lose weight: eat less and exercise more. In my family, my mom, sister, and I bonded with our unhealthy eating habits. My mom died at 76 after 12 years in a wheelchair as a result of a stroke. My sister Marti was only 50 years old when she died of high blood pressure. The day I found Marti deceased in her home in 2007 was the most devastating day of my life. I turned to food for comfort, and I soared to over 220 pounds. I discovered inner strength and optimism through my connection to my higher power, finding comfort and purpose.

I have a coach for my nutrition. I ask myself each time I hire my coach, "What if I don't know the answers?" Coming from the mindset of not knowing, I am open to learning and transforming my nutrition.

What works for me is a daily plan to eat a certain amount of the macro food groups of proteins, carbs, and fat. Whole real foods. I plan my meals every day, putting everything into MyFitnessPal or Trainerize, and hitting my goals of grams and calories daily. I take my daily supplements, drink 100-120 ounces of water daily, and manage stress. Sleep is the most critical, 7-8 hours daily. I had a paradigm shift around food. Now, I live by the "eat to live" mindset versus my family's pattern of eating, which was "live to eat."

Spirituality

Praying to my higher power is part of my daily routine. The serenity prayer is one of my mantras. "God, grant me the serenity to accept the things I cannot change, the courage to change the things I can, and the wisdom to know the difference." Judaism, for me, is spiritual, religious, and cultural. In my meditation practice, I incorporate Buddhism and Native American Indian spirituality—a holistic approach to wellness through body, mind, and spirit.

Fitness

Just a little cardio for me includes walking for 30 minutes 5 days a week, and strength training 3-5 days a week for 35-50 minutes. I work out at home with block weights, resistance bands, TRX, a yoga mat, and a foam roller. I have just added the 48" rebounder trampoline to my workouts. I play pickleball 2-3 times a week and coach pickleball 3-4 days a week.

Ownership

Owning all my life, the good, the bad, and the ugly. Being with what is so. Not blaming myself or others. Not making myself or others wrong. When

I own it all, that gives me all the power. Not being a victim. Grace with myself.

Responsibility

"Responsibility includes efficiently completing tasks." Being responsible, as a possibility. We are entrusted with realizing something's potential, turning its promise into reality. Being and living powerfully.

Mindfulness

The practice of being aware of your thoughts, feelings, and surroundings in the present moment without judgment. Present in this moment now. Be here now. Mindful living. Mindful eating. Mindful self-care. There is nothing to "maintain." We get to create our lives every day, every moment.

"The secret of health for both mind and body is not to mourn for the past, nor to worry about the future, but to live the present moment wisely and earnestly." ~ Buddha

Lisa is an inspirational leader, coach ("Coach Lisa"), author, speaker, healer, athlete, artist, juggler, owner of Lisa Frumhoff Real Estate / Berkshire Hathaway HomeServices Alliance Real Estate (Licensed Realtor® in Missouri since 1994), and a Five Star Real Estate Agent award winner multiple years. She is also an advisor, consultant, negotiator, and Dual Certified Pickleball Pro Instructor PPR and IPTPA.

Lisa has earned 30+ pickleball medals as a player, including the U.S. Open silver medal and regional championship gold, silver, and bronze medals. She has competed in the USA Pickleball National Championships for 3+ years, earning 4th place in singles. She's also competed in the Pickleball World Championships. Lisa played in the 1994 Gay Games in New York and won a gold medal in softball. She played in the National Sports Festival and played on the 1985 Women's North Regional soccer team. Lisa is an All-America soccer goalkeeper and an international bestselling author for her chapter, "Real Connections Matter" in *The Anatomy of Accomplishment*. Lisa is an Athletic Hall of Fame inductee two times at Missouri S&T in Rolla, Missouri—in 2002 for being the school's first woman soccer player and in 2012 for the 1983 soccer team.

Lisa is the co-owner of Energize Pickleball. She is also an Energy Clearer, Certified Reiki Master, Reiki I, II, III, and Mastery. She is an artist and creator of udu drums.

Please scan the QR code to connect with this author.

RESOURCE LISTINGS

jgoptimalwellness.com

We help women achieve optimal health by educating, empowering, and addressing the root causes of symptoms to support overall wellness and long-term well-being.

JG *Optimal Wellness*

Disease is inevitable. Health is not!

---

womenofasphalt.org

Women of Asphalt is a national organization empowering women in the asphalt industry through mentorship, education, networking, and advocacy to promote growth and leadership opportunities.

Empowering Women in Asphalt Industry Careers

I share my journey to inspire others to ignite their curiosity, embrace challenges with courage, and harness their inner strength to forge their unique paths to success.

Kristen Ziegler
Your story is your strength.

RESOURCE LISTINGS

linkedin.com/in/cheryl-houston

Inspiring others to use credible resources, radical hope, and sometimes curious choices as a path through challenging circumstances, one step and one breath at a time.

Cheryl A. Houston PhD, CHES, RDN, LD, FAND

---

moverecoaching.com

We empower leaders, professionals, and teams to unlock their strengths, lead authentically, and create thriving workplaces through coaching, leader development, and team effectiveness solutions.

Empowering Talent. Maximizing Strengths. Creating Momentum.

---

gadellnet.com

Our dedicated team of IT specialists provides tailored technology solutions like 24/7 help desk support, cybersecurity, strategic consulting, and project management services.

RESOURCE LISTINGS

halconmarketing.com

Drawing on over ten decades of combined experience, we propel your brand to the next level by harnessing our innate creative talents with cutting-edge neuromarketing, psychology, and market research.

H Λ L C O N

We build POWERFUL and PROFITABLE brands.

---

linkedin.com/in/juliekappen

A proactive partner always looking out for the best interest of my clients. Focused on bringing creative solutions to curb healthcare spend.

"Those who have no time for healthy eating will sooner or later have to find the time for illness." – Edward Stanley

---

krilogy.com

Our approach to financial management is based on the core values of dedication, abundance, leadership and respect. We are your trusted wealth management partner and are committed to serving you and your family.

KRILOGY.

Helping people live their best lives and achieve their financial dreams.

RESOURCE LISTINGS

prospercpas.com

Prosper CPAs is a full-service CPA firm serving professionals and service industries. Our award-winning accounting professionals share these beliefs: offer industry-leading fresh perspectives and premium service.

Experienced Professionals. Fresh Ideas.

---

bumblebeeblinds.com

We're buzzing about beautiful window treatments that make your home a sanctuary. We do the work and take care of the details while you showcase your style and sense of design.

BUMBLE BEE BLINDS™

Your Vision. Our Expertise.

---

daffneymoore.com/icg/

From adversity to advocacy, I share my journey in turning personal setbacks into powerful comebacks through leadership and resilience. Let me help you achieve the same.

INNOVATIVE CONSULTING GROUP

Resilience Redefined: Turning Setbacks into Comebacks

RESOURCE LISTINGS

united4children.org

United 4 Children is dedicated to elevating and supporting early childhood educators, children, and families so that they can thrive across the state of Missouri.

Every child has the foundation to thrive

---

marthashands.com

For 27 years, families have chosen Martha's Hands Home Care Services to assist their loved ones with their daily activities and support. We deliver care based on our mission of Love through Service.

Compassion and Excellence in Health Care

---

purehonestwater.com

Join Honest Water's community! We provide affordable, purified drinking water to Southern Illinois and St. Louis Metro, prioritizing reliability and access for all.

H₂ONEST WATER

CLEAN. PURE. HONEST.

RESOURCE LISTINGS

higherstateconsulting.com

Success is a natural result of improving your internal State of Mind. Learn to manage more work at a higher quality and be able to walk away quietly at the end of the day.

---

bjzrealty.com

We are the "Concierge of Real Estate." Our service to the client base here at the BJZ Real Estate Collective is of the highest level. Bringing the client education and delivering customer care, is our daily goal.

BJZ Real Estate Collective by BJZRealty LLC
Buy, Sell, Invest, call the best!

---

rrmarketplace.org

The R&R Marketplace is an epicenter of change, serving individuals and families in the region through workforce development, early childhood education, financial empowerment, and entrepreneurial advancement.

www.ingramcontent.com/pod-product-compliance
Lightning Source LLC
Chambersburg PA
CBHW071148130626
46553CB00004B/1567